BAND WEAVING

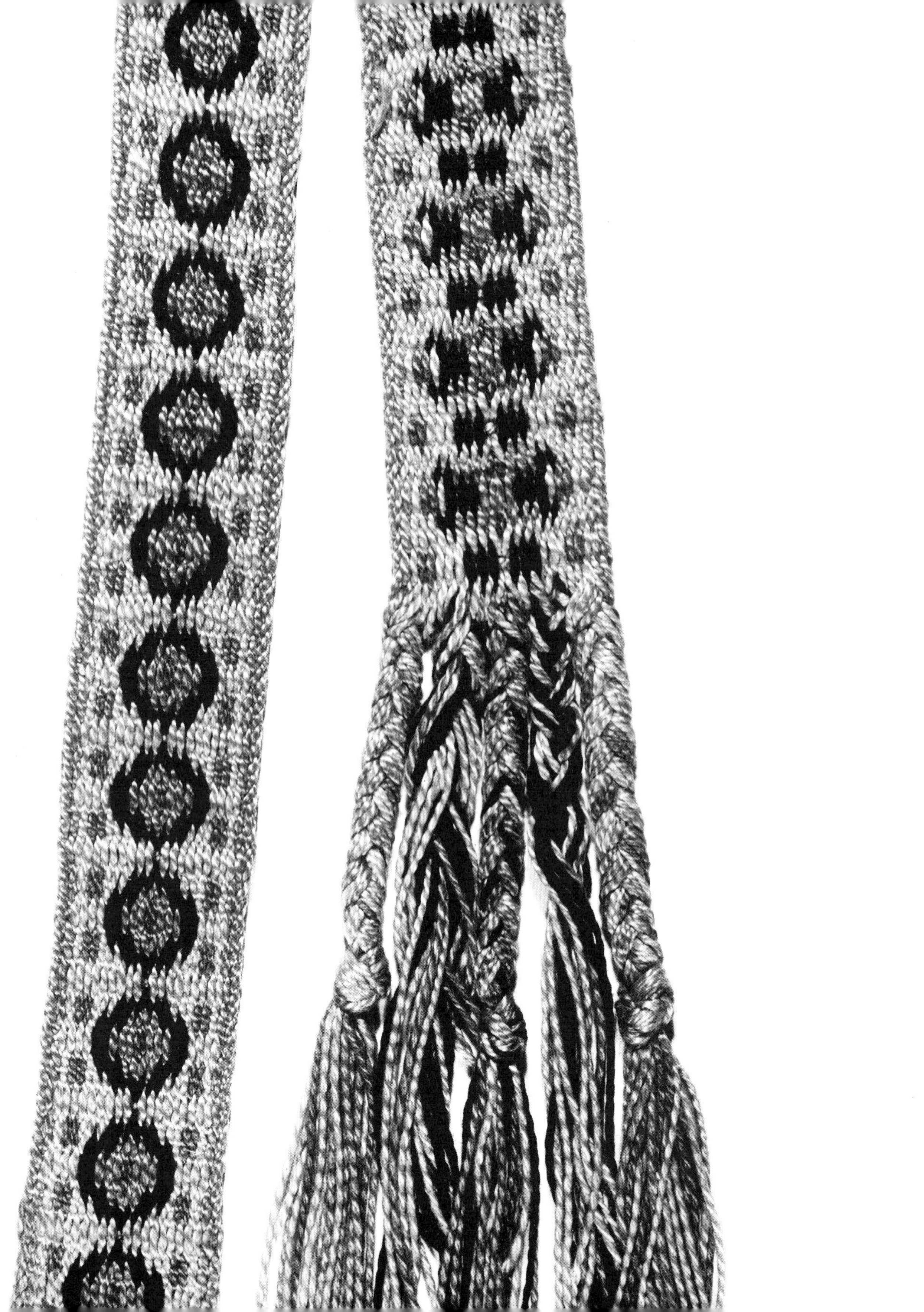

BAND WEAVING

The Techniques, Looms, and Uses for Woven Bands

Harold and Sylvia Tacker

VNR VAN NOSTRAND REINHOLD COMPANY
New York Cincinnati Toronto London Melbourne

Lovingly dedicated to our two daughters, Jo Ann and Meegan

Acknowledgments

As we wrote this book it became increasingly apparent that every contact we had had with weavers, museums, schools, and books had been of invaluable assistance in the preparation and production of the final work. We wish we could give proper thanks to all those people we touched in passing.

Fresh in our memory are the ones who gave so much of their time, their thoughts, and their efforts generously, patiently, and with great understanding this past year. Our deep appreciation goes to the weavers who shared their weaving and so freely gave their time to create pieces especially for us.

We are particularly indebted to Erna Aasheim and Dr. Marta Hoffman of Oslo, Norway, and to Peter Collingwood in England who took time to help two strangers. Many thanks go to Alette Skille and Mabel Gutzler, whose graphic and expressive translations of Scandinavian weaving books opened the doors of the history of band weaving to us. We are most grateful to Gertrude Mortensen for her congenial criticism and to Jean Knox for her typing skills.

The task of doing illustrations to accompany the instructions fell to our friend, Lois Keeler, whose clear-cut drawings take over when the limitations of the written word require it.

We were fortunate to be able to avail ourselves of the photographic skills of Kent Kammerer and William Eng, and we are especially grateful to Helga and Ernest Fortescue for many extra hours of photographic endeavor. Many thanks to the unfailingly courteous and helpful Diane Sugimura and Virginia Harvey for letting us browse through the Textile and Costume Study Center at the University of Washington and to Fred and Leslie Hart of La Tienda Imports in Seattle who most generously made their textile treasures available for photographing.

We are indebted to Estelle Silbermann for her conscientious editing and her personal encouragement. Finally, our very special thanks to Jean Wilson, whose encouraging words prompted this book.

ALL DRAWINGS ARE BY LOIS KEELER WITH THE EXCEPTION OF THE PATTERN DRAFTS, WHICH WERE DONE BY THE AUTHORS.

Van Nostrand Reinhold Company Regional Offices:
New York Cincinnati Chicago Millbrae Dallas
Van Nostrand Reinhold Co. International Offices:
London Toronto Melbourne

Copyright © 1974 by Litton Educational Publishing, Inc.
Library of Congress Catalog Card Number: 73–1633
ISBN: 0–442–28404–7

All rights reserved. No part of this work covered by the copyright hereon may be reproduced or used in any form or by any means — graphic, electronic, or mechanical, including photocopying, recording, taping, or information storage and retrieval systems — without written permission of the publisher. Manufactured in the United States of America.

Designed By Elaine Gongora

Published by Van Nostrand Reinhold Company
A Division of Litton Educational Publishing, Inc.
450 West 33rd Street, New York, N. Y. 10001

16 15 14 13 12 11 10 9 8 7 6 5 4 3 2 1

Library of Congress Cataloging in Publication Data

Tacker, Harold, 1910-
  Band weaving.

  Bibliography: p.
  1. Hand weaving. I. Tacker, Sylvia, 1919- joint author. II. Title.
TT848.T25   746.1'4   73–1633
ISBN 0–442–28404–7

contents

	Acknowledgments	4
1.	Introduction	6
2.	A Brief History and General Weaving Instructions	8
3.	Simple Finger-Woven Bands	14
4.	Soda-Straw Loom Bands	18
5.	Hungarian-Loom Bands	20
6.	Twining-Loom Bands	26
7.	Rigid-Heddle Bands	32
8.	Band Weaving on the American Inkle Loom	54
9.	Card-Woven Bands	64
10.	Weaving Variations for Special Effects	76
	List of Suppliers	101
	Bibliography	102
	Index	103
	Photo Credits	104

1. introduction

In all of us there is an inborn desire to create, a desire which often lies dormant, but which now, in the midst of a prefabricated world, seems to have been aroused almost as though in self-defense against this world. Today's resurgence of hand weaving in general, and lately of band weaving in particular, is another emphatic sign of this search for individuality.

We gain deep satisfaction from producing something shaped with our own hands from start to finish. In our time we can use our handcrafts to express our own originality and imagination. And if what we create is also functional, then we add another dimension to our weaving. Since industrial weaving provides adequate and economical textiles, we are left free to lend richness and originality to these textiles with hand-woven touches such as bands. Best of all, band weaving can be a take-along leisure pastime, one which can help us to relax and which we can pursue without a deadline.

This book was written for both the experienced weaver who wants to enrich her weaving craft and for the beginning weaver who wishes to learn a useful and imaginative handcraft. Band weaving can be as simple or complicated as you want to make it. The looms themselves are portable, take little storage space, and are inexpensive to build or buy.

There are so many varied uses for bands. Use them alone as trim, belts, bookmarks, dog collars, suspenders, cords for jewelry, bellpulls, or straps for bags. Join them to another weaving to widen the piece as well as to add decoration. Or join them to each other and make pillows, bags, ponchos, afghans, or bedspreads. A bedspread won't be made in a week, but band by band it can develop into an incomparable heirloom. (See Figure 10–15.)

In a less functional vein, bands can be added to wall hangings and tapestries or they may compose the hanging itself. You can even make a band-woven doll. (See Figure 10–39.) This list still doesn't cover all of the possibilities, but we hope that the examples in the following pages and the numerous photographs will give you a good idea of the many ways to use woven bands.

In Chapter 2 a brief history of band weaving is followed by definitions of the basic terms you will need if you are a beginning weaver. There will be instructions on how to start a band so as to make an end that won't unravel, a description of band-weaving tools, and general instructions on the way to weave a band.

In Chapter 3 you will find some simple instructions for basic finger weaving. Chapters 4, 5, and 6 describe band weaving on some small looms you can make yourself, without any special tools: the soda straw loom, and the Hungarian and twining looms. These looms can be used by teachers, activity directors, baby sitters, mothers, and hobby weavers to entertain themselves and to teach others how to weave.

Chapters 7 and 8 explain the use of some of the more complicated looms — the rigid heddle and American inkle loom — which can be made with the help of woodworking tools or can be purchased from the loom supply sources listed at the end of the book. In Chapter 9 you will learn how to weave with cards. The final chapter will show you how to add distinctive or practical touches to your weaving with wrapped warps, weaving slits for decoration or buttonholes, weft insertions, and other techniques.

For each loom we have included some threading or weaving drafts to give you additional ideas for band weaving designs. You will soon begin to have ideas for your own patterns after you have tried the ones we suggest. Similarly, all the instructions for threading, weaving, warping, and other specific techniques will be your basic methods, your essential starting points. Follow the instructions once or twice, but from then on don't hesitate to improve upon, simplify, or add to the procedure outlined for each weaving device. Using your imagination may take practice, but you will find to your delight that you have more of it than you thought.

2.
a brief history and general weaving instructions

Band weaving is a very ancient craft. Woven ribbons or bands have been uncovered throughout the world, some apparently having been used as marks of identification or of status, as symbols of attainment, or to serve the more mundane functions of sandal straps, garment fastenings, and harnesses or yokes for transporting heavy loads.

Costly card-woven bands made of spun silk and gold were used in the eighth and ninth centuries for trim on chasubles and other religious vestments and were considered proof of the status of the wearer. In some of the Scandinavian countries, specific colors and designs of woven and embroidered bands denoted the region or county of origin. Bits of woven bands have been found in graves more than a thousand years old in the northern parts of Scandinavia. This is the land over which the Laplanders roamed, and their people are buried here. Because of the construction of the graves and the nature of the earth, many pieces of woven fabric were preserved.

The Lapland woman might have woven her bands as she watched over the family herd of reindeer. Striking her herding staff into the ground, she could attach one end of her coarse wool threads to it and stretch the other to a stout birch tree branch, then twist the fibers into strong bands to use as shoelaces, carrying straps, or trimming for headgear. These early bands may have been composed of only warp or lengthwise threads and were woven without the aid of weaving tools. Fibers were looped over a tree branch and the weaver used her fingers to twist, knot, braid, or plait them. No binding or weft fiber was used in these single-element techniques.

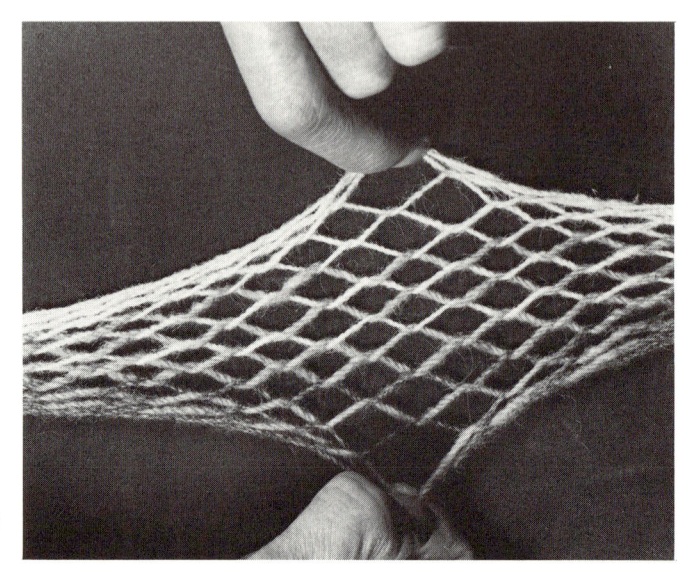

2-1. Note the twisted elastic mesh of the weftless technique in a sprang band.

Greek and Peruvian fragments dating back to 1500 B.C. show plait work of different kinds and the Egyptians used sprang to make stockings for the pharoahs. Sprang can best be described as a method of twisting fibers around each other to produce a strong knotless mesh giving the appearance of a fish net. *Sprang: Thread Twisting, a Creative Textile Technique,* by Hella Skowronski and Mary Reddy, describes this technique thoroughly. (See the Bibliography.)

Prehistoric Pueblo Indians used braiding or finger weaving for sashes as well as tumplines and straps. (Figure 2–2 shows a contemporary finger-woven sash.) Extremely narrow bands have been brought to light during research into ancient clothing in Sweden. These bands were used on clothing that had to be washed in place of metal fastenings which would rust.

2-2. The braided sash detail was designed and woven by Marty Holm.

Textiles found in prehistoric graves were woven in the Iron and Bronze Ages by means of a weaving process identical to the card weaving method that is used today. However, the ancient cards, called tablets, were constructed of wood, stiffened hide, bone, or horn shaped into squares with a hole drilled in each corner of each square. Occasionally a set of cards has been found still attached to the unfinished band,

2-3. This card weaving was discovered in an ancient burial mound among the Oseberg findings. (Courtesy Universitetets Oldsaksamling, Oslo, Norway.)

the handwork of the woman buried with her, perhaps to keep her busy on her journey ahead.

Thus the tradition of band weaving is apparently a long and honorable one. Now we come back to the present to give those of you who have never woven before some fundamental information you will need before you begin to weave your own band.

Weaving might be defined as the interlacing of threads to form a fabric. In braiding or plaiting, only one set of threads is intertwined to make the fabric. However, when band-weaving looms are used, there are two sets of threads. One set of *warp* or lengthwise threads is bound together to form a solid fabric by means of a binding or *weft* thread. The weaving is accomplished by separating two layers of alternate warp threads to provide a space in which to place the weft threads. This space is called a *shed*. To "change the shed" means to exchange the upper layer of threads for those on the lower layer. The two sets of threads are interchanged throughout the weaving, each time creating a new opening for the weft. The loom devices enable you to make these shed changes.

A woven band is a long and narrow warp-faced fabric, "warp-faced" meaning that the warp yarns are packed close together so that the binding thread or weft is hidden, except at the edge of the band where it makes a turn to go into the

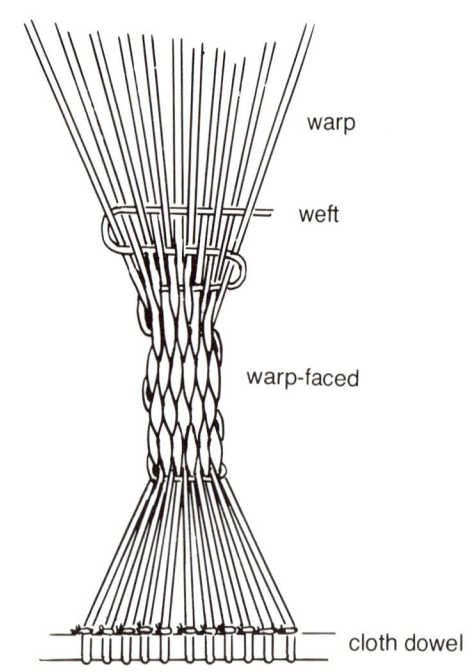

2-4. The basic construction of the woven band: warp threads and the hidden weft produce a warp-faced fabric.

next shed. Each passage of the weft through the shed is called a *shot*. The warp threads in band weaving are held under tension in some way by the loom, and the arrangement of these warp threads, by color and sequence, sets the pattern of the band. The weft may also be called "woof" or "binding threads."

The tools you will use are looms, shuttles, heddles, cards, bobbins, and your fingers. For the purpose of band weaving, a *loom* is any device which will hold a number of threads in a stationary position and keep them in the order in which they were threaded or "warped" to this device. The main reason for having a loom, in addition to controlling the order of the threads, is to provide you with a method of controlling the tension of each warp thread.

Man's first attempts at weaving were with his fingers and his materials in those days were strips of bark and plant fibers. Looms were developed eventually through trial and error. As spinning developed and man's requirements for woven fabrics became more sophisticated, a weaving method that could be faster and perhaps more accurate needed to be developed.

The invention of the *heddle* made possible the true loom. A device for the mechanical manipulation of the warp threads, the heddle can be made of string, metal, or wood, just as long as it has a hole or eye through which the warp thread may be passed, and which will control that single warp thread throughout the weaving. In these pages we will be describing string heddles, which are used on the inkle loom (see Chapter 8), and the rigid heddle, which is a frame that can be made all in one piece and that has vertical slits and holes in the solid areas between the slits (see Chapter 7).

The threads are held taut and even throughout the course of weaving by means of tension. If you keep the threads evenly tight while you weave, you will have a firm, uniform band. In band weaving, weft tension is also very important. Each time the weft is passed through the shed it should be pulled up against the warp edge, known as the "selvedge," with the exact amount of tension or pull as in the previous weft shot. Since this requires attention even from experienced weavers, use a gauge, like a knitting stitch gauge, or make a template from a piece of cardboard cut or marked to the correct measurement of the width of the band. (Figure 2–5.)

2-5. You can use an emery board to gauge and maintain uniform width. A slight advantage is that the board will to some extent adhere to the fibers.

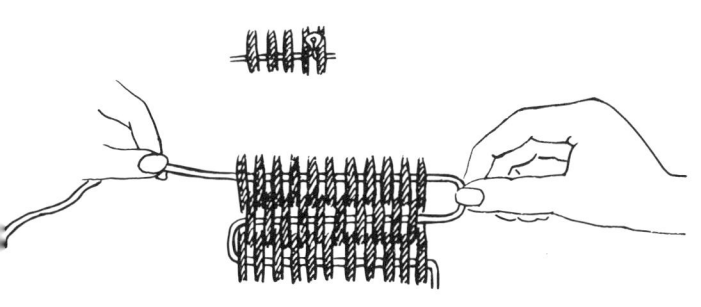

2-6. The weft loop goes into place against the selvedge. The small drawing on top shows how a thread "bubbles" if it is not pulled snugly to the warp edge.

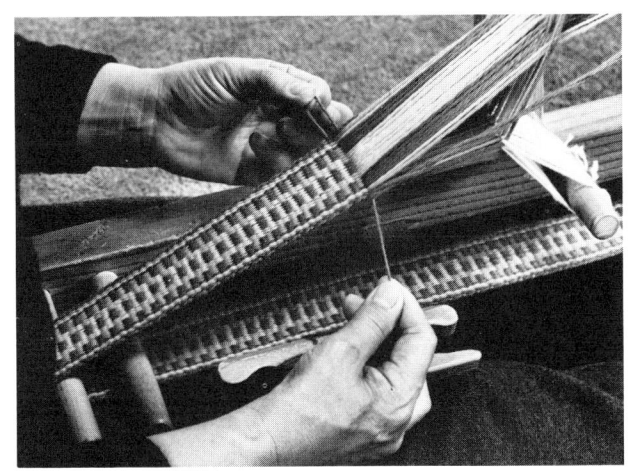

2-7. The correct way to guide the weft through the shed.

Another aid in keeping a firm, uniform edge on the band is to draw the weft thread through the shed in such a way that it doesn't form a loop between the two outside threads. (Figures 2–6 and 2–7.) One way to do this is to catch the weft thread with your finger as it makes the turn for the next shot. Then when you put your shuttle carrying the weft from one side of the warp to the other, through the shed, the finger holding the weft thread can control it so that it will slide in smoothly and snugly against the outside warp only. You will actually be finishing the pull-in on the previous shot as you carry out this process.

The *shuttle* is a yarn carrier or holder for the weft threads as you weave. There are many different types of shuttles. (Figure 2–8.) Those for band weaving can be made short and for wider weavings they can be made longer. A belt shuttle has a knife edge on one side to facilitate "beating." (See p. 13.) We have also started using bobbins in Hungarian band weaving since they help in identifying the two sets of warp

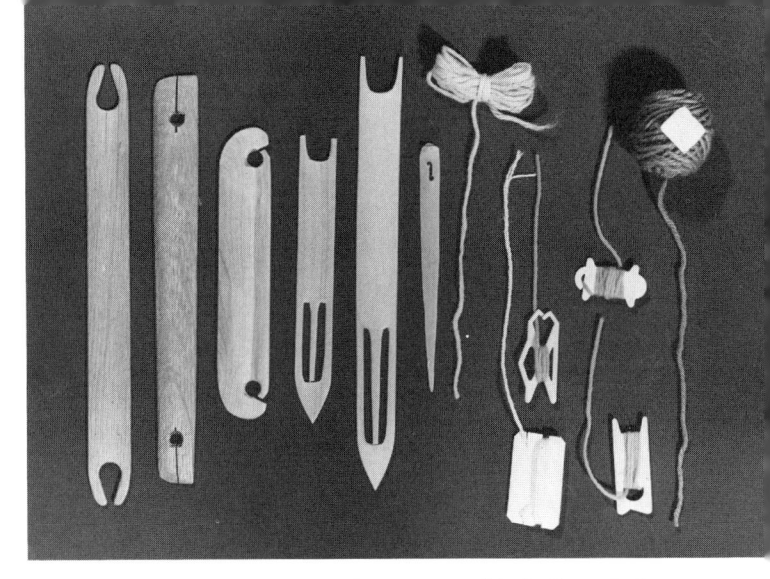

2-8. From left to right the yarn carriers are: two stick shuttles, a belt shuttle, two netting shuttles, a pick-up needle, a butterfly (see *Figure 2-9*), several bobbins used for finger weaving and Hungarian loom warp yarns, and a ball of weft yarn in which the thread feeds from the center of the ball and masking tape secures the other end.

that are exchanged to produce the woven band, and keep beginners from tangling the warps. (See Chapter 5.) This is especially helpful when working with schoolchildren.

A butterfly is made on the palm of the hand. (Figure 2–9.) You hold the starting end of the yarn by the thumb against the hand. The yarn is then looped around the thumb, goes across the palm and behind the little finger. On its return trip the yarn comes around the little finger, crosses in the center, and goes behind the thumb, making a figure eight. When a suitable amount of yarn has been wound, cut the yarn and, using this last cut end, wind it around the cross, making certain that the beginning piece of yarn is caught in the wrapping. End the wrap with a knotted loop, pulled tight to keep the wrap from unraveling.

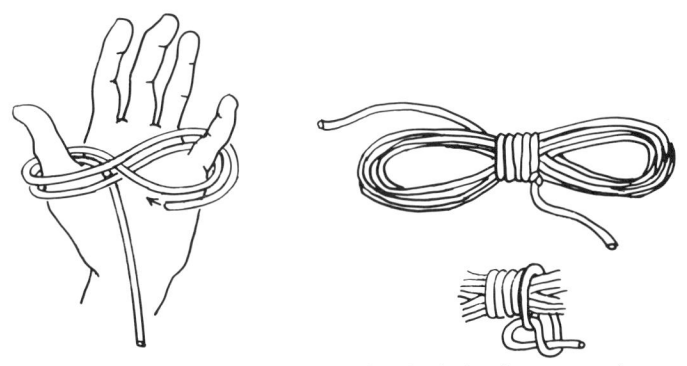

2-9. A butterfly can be used in place of a shuttle for short spans of weaving — for example, in weaving a slit for a short distance in a band (See page 76.)

11

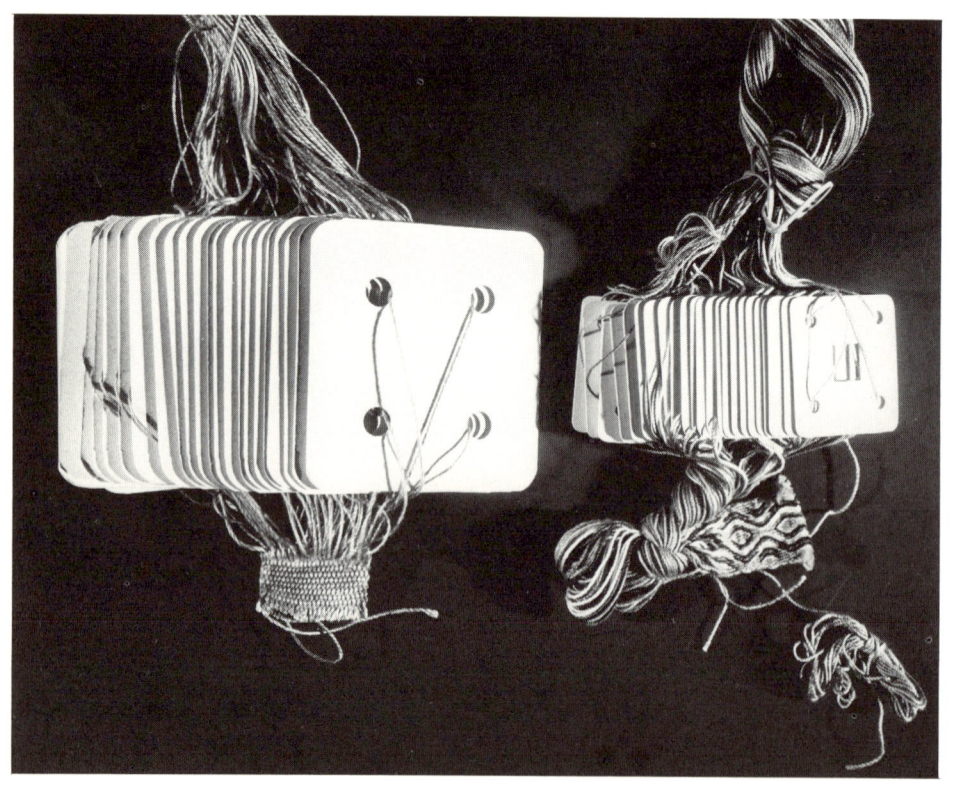

2-10. Two styles of commercial cards: the cards on the left are of heavy cardboard, those on the right of plastic. (From the Harriet Tidball collection, Courtesy of the Costume and Textile Study Center, School of Home Economics, University of Washington.)

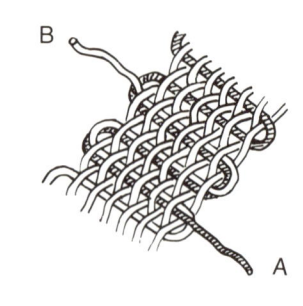

2-11. The new weft is inserted at point A and carried along with the old weft for three shots to point B, where the old weft ends and can be snipped off.

The cards used for card weaving are thin, square plates made of cardboard or plastic. Each card has four holes, one in each corner. There are departures from this form. For example, some cards have a fifth hole in the center and there are cards with round or hexagonal shapes. However, since the square four-holed cards are made by several manufacturers and easy to purchase, we will be limiting ourselves to their use.

As for the weaving itself, to start, wind plenty of weft on your shuttle so you won't have to splice new weft as you go. It is difficult to determine how much weft you will need, since yarns vary, the beat down will be different for different weavers, and the weft tension or pull-in will vary; therefore you should wind a good full shuttle.

After you have threaded the warps, you open the shed and make the first shot, leaving a tail of yarn about four or five inches long. Then with the next four or five shots and shed changes, tuck the tail piece in along with the weft until it is all woven in. This procedure will form an end selvedge so that it will not be necessary for you to stitch along the end of the band to keep it from raveling. If you run out of weft yarn before the band is finished, you should start a new weft while there are still three or four shots left on the old one. Do not tie a knot in the two wefts; it will show in the woven band. Lay the new weft in the same shed as the old weft and with each shed change and shot, carry the two wefts along until the old one is used up. (Figure 2–11.) This is essentially what you did when you began your weaving. Then you can clip off any bits of weft ends that remain sticking out. Just one word of caution: Be sure that the tension is the same for both new and old weft as you splice. When you purchase a loom, you will also get specific instructions on starting, weaving, and finishing the bands on that particular loom.

To produce a uniform, firm, and pleasing band you must

pay attention to the "beat" you use in weaving. Beating describes the action of pressing or packing a weft shot firmly against the previous weaving. With each shed change, the beat is made in the empty shed and pressed against the previous shot before you lay in the new weft. (Figures 2–12 and 2–13.) You can beat with the side of your hand or with the edge of the shuttle. The beat determines the firmness and the eventual overall length of each pattern. Tight, firm beating takes up more of the warp during weaving than looser beating.

There are more detailed definitions available in other books on weaving, but essentially this is all that is needed to follow our instructions for band weaving. The specific weaving instructions for each loom will be found in the chapter covering the particular loom.

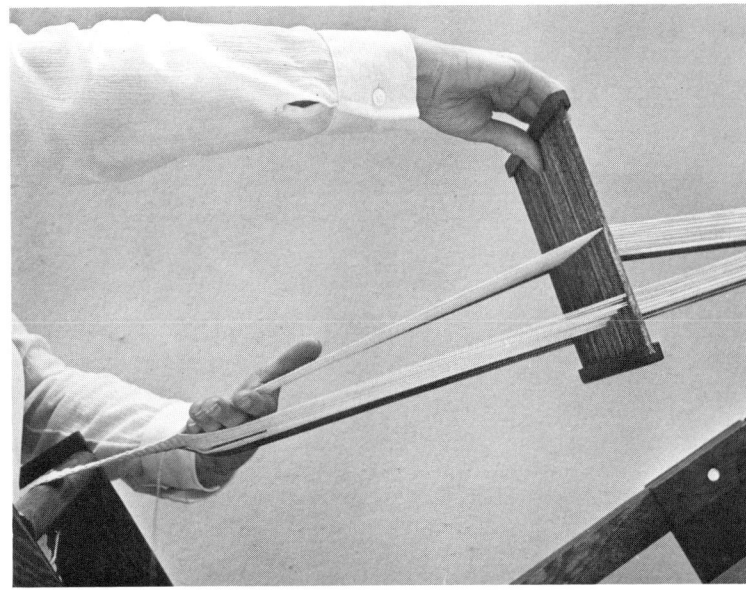

2-12. With a strong blow, the side of the hand strikes the weft and beats it firmly against the previous wefts.

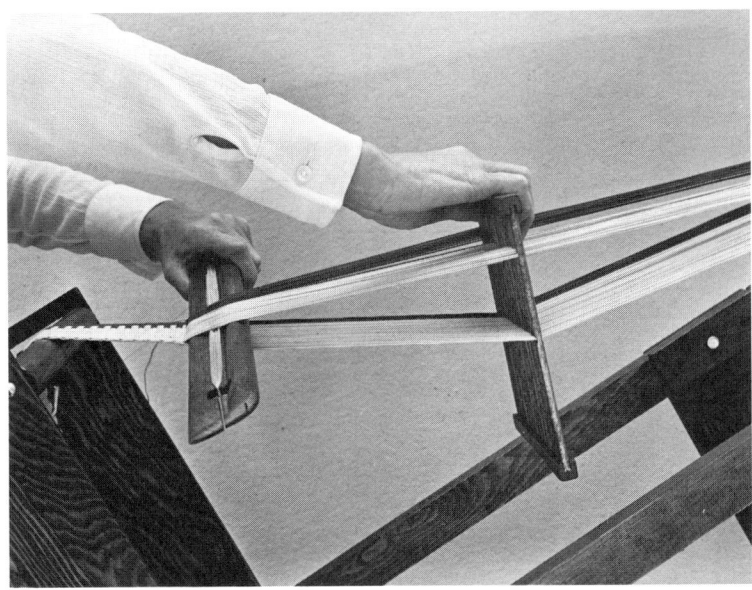

2-13. The shuttle edge is an equally effective beater.

3.
simple finger-woven bands

The most immediate weaving tools are the fingers of your hands. Evidence gathered concerning early man shows that his first attempts at weaving took the form of plaited strips of bark and grasses and finger-woven bands. In North America, these forms of weaving were known to a people who flourished more than two thousand years ago in the Southwest and whom historians have named "the Basketmakers."

Plaiting more nearly resembles loom weaving, which in effect is mechanical plaiting, the over and under of two fibers to form a fabric. Braiding, sometimes called finger weaving, is also one of the more simple, primitive weaving methods and requires no tools except skillful fingers. It can be done with a minimum of three strands of fiber, but there are no limits to the number of yarns that can be braided. Using this technique, some of the early Indian tribes manipulated hundreds of yarns to make their ceremonial sashes. Figure 3-1 shows a contemporary interpretation of the ceremonial sash design. The type of long sash shown in Figure 3-1 is started in the middle. One half is woven, then the sash is turned and the other half is woven. The two sticks are lashed together to hold the center of the strands in place and to keep tension while the braid is being woven.

Simple four-strand braids might have a variety of uses: they could serve as bag handles, tie belts, edgings for pillows, and trim for a number of things. They may also be used as finishings for belts, rugs, or wall hangings. Suitable yarns for finger weaving are perle and rug cotton, rug wool, fingering yarn, worsted wools, jute, heavy carpet linen, and acrylic yarns.

A four-strand braid that is easy to do is shown in Figure 3-2. Notice how the bobbins help to control the yarns and the two nails at one end of the board serve as a hitching post to help maintain tension. Practice the braid a couple of times using short strands of thick yarn. Then plan a project which can employ a band like this — such as a tie belt or tote bag

3-1. This contemporary Osage-style braiding was woven by Bill Holm.

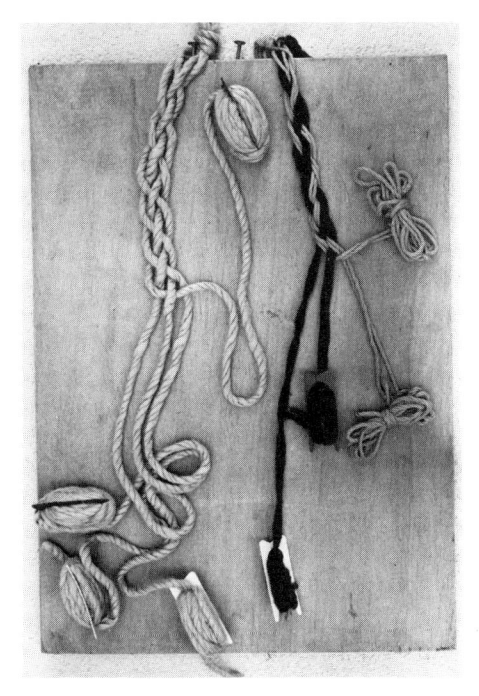

3-2. A simple four-strand braid.

3-3. The bags were woven by Harriette Gardner.

handle. Figure 3–3 shows two ideas for bag handles. In the bag on the left, the handle was woven in (see Figure 3–5), while the handle for the tote bag on the right was sewn on along the two sides.

To weave your band, first measure the amount of yarn you will need for your bag handle; for the average tote bag you will need at least three and one-half to four yards of braid. Allow extra yarn for all your weaving, since it is difficult to add on yarn but easy to cut it off.

Cut four strands of rug cotton three and one-half yards long. We used a lofty cotton about one quarter inch in diameter. If you use a lighter-weight rug yarn, double it for each strand.

Tie the top of all four strands together in a secure knot and then fasten it to a hitching post. Plan to have some sort of work surface on which to lay the threads while you braid. You may use a clipboard, a couple of nails pounded in a board, or a piece of strong tape to hold the yarns for you, because you do pull them a little while you weave, so you need to provide some sort of tensioning.

As mentioned earlier, when the strands are long and rather unmanageable, you can wind them on bobbins. You can make your own bobbins out of cardboard or use argyle bobbins. Or else you can wind the strands into butterflies before you tie them together in the first knot. (See page 11 and Figure 2–9.)

Now study the directions of the left braid's first thread as it weaves over and under the other three in Figure 3–2. Begin at the outside of the left side. Lift the outside thread up from the left and weave it over and under and over across the band. Pull it tight enough to bring all the threads together closely. Then lay it *up* on the right side.

Pick up the outside thread from the left side once more and repeat the weaving across to the right. Bring the first thread *down* to be woven in and lay the second thread *up* on the right side the same way you did with thread number one.

Always take the outside thread from the same side of the braid. This same method may be used for braids made of many more strands of yarn and braids may also be woven from right to left. If you start from the left, weave the entire band from the left side, and if you start from the right side, continue from the right side all the way. When the band is finished, tie the ends into a knot or bind them with a strong thread so that they won't come apart.

15

3-4. The eight-strand braid was woven from one side only — this time the right side.

3-6. For this type of pattern, always cross the two center threads before you start braiding.

If you are weaving a bag on a two- or four-harness loom, Figure 3–5 shows how to weave the handle in as part of the bag.

For the precise steps to follow, you might weave four inches of the bag, then lay in the braid just as you would any weft, leaving an equal amount of braid hanging out each side.

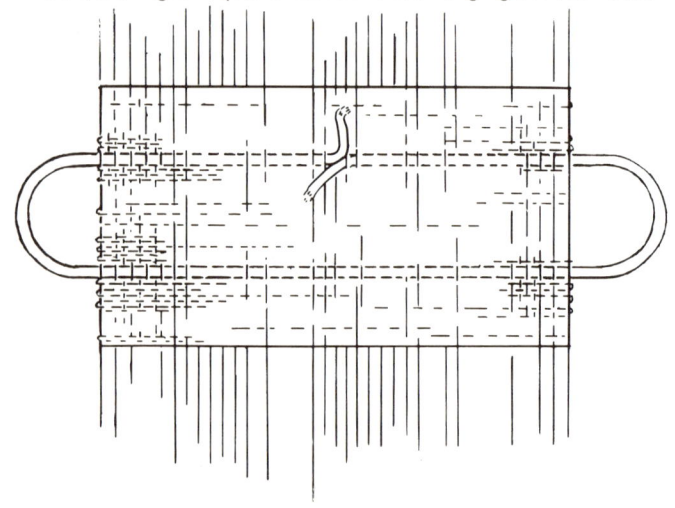

3-5. Weaving in a braid or any handle with the weft.

Weave six more inches of the bag and then bring the ends of the braided handle back into the open shed with the ends meeting and slightly overlapping.

After you finish weaving the bag, tie the ends of the braid carefully one by one to each other on the wrong side of the work so they will not come apart in use. If the bag is lined, the knotted ends will never show. If your band is to be fastened onto a bag which is already woven or is made of commercially woven fabric, the handle may be whipped or sewn on the bag.

To give another kind of pattern to the weaving, you could try using eight strands and weave your belt or handle like the one in Figure 3–6. You would repeat the measuring and cutting steps as in the previous project as well as the instructions for winding the bobbins and setting up some sort of tensioning device, a hitching post.

Then, take the two center threads, cross them, and start one thread *under* and the other thread *over* the adjacent yarns and continue weaving over and under alternate threads to the outside of each side. Lay the threads up on the outsides until the next two threads are woven across; then lay them down in place to be woven in.

To weave the finger-woven belt in Figure 3–7 you need

16

3-7. This finger-woven belt is made by moving warp yarns from one side only, as in Figure 3–4. (Student work under the instruction of Inge Buley.)

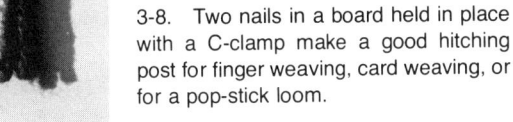

3-8. Two nails in a board held in place with a C-clamp make a good hitching post for finger weaving, card weaving, or for a pop-stick loom.

3-9. A lark's head hitch.

3-10. Some of the end fringes of this Turkish sash are braided; others are wrapped with horse hair tassels. This idea could be expanded into a three-dimensional design. (Courtesy of Fred and Leslie Hart.)

heavy wool, cotton, or rayon rug yarn or jute. Determine the finished length of the belt and add one-fourth more yarn for weaving take-up and fringe.

You can hook the buckle over a nail in the manner shown in Figure 3–8. Cut three strands of light-colored yarn and two strands of dark-colored yarn twice the length you need. Fold the yarns in half and loop them one by one over the buckle. One way to do this is to make a lark's head or ring hitch. Fold the looped end of the yarn over the buckle or ring and tuck both free ends of the yarn through the loop, pulling them down tight against the buckle. (Figure 3–9).

The weaving, which progresses from the buckle toward you, is done in the same manner as the first braid, from one side only. This time you are weaving with ten strands instead of four, but the method is the same. Push the weaving thread up against the buckle so that the belt will be strong and firm. To finish the belt you can tie the fringes in paired knots or you might add a small bead and then a knot.

Projects involving simple four-strand finger weaving are suitable for children. More complicated braiding, however, is liable to be baffling to them.

4.
soda-straw loom bands

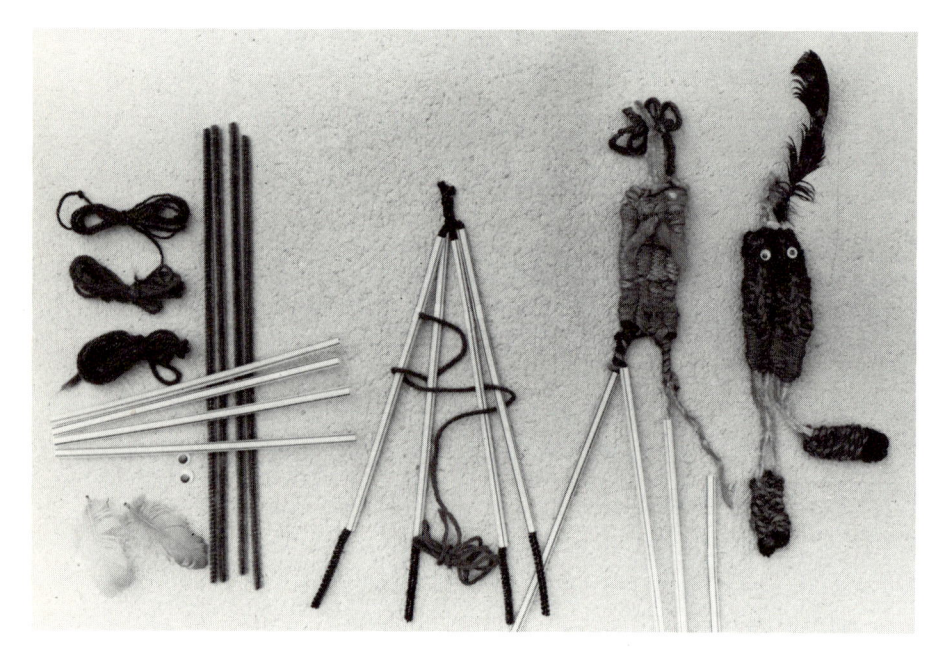

4-1. Shown from left to right are: the materials for one soda straw band; the straws threaded with pipe cleaner warps; removing the straws from the weaving; the finished doll on which has been sewn two small braid "suspenders" and with shoes and socks that were woven using the pipe cleaners without the straws, in pairs, as the loom, and weaving over and under to cover the "feet."

Weaving with the soda-straw loom can be very elementary, but this procedure can also become too complicated for children when more than six straws are used with long warps. In its simplest form, however, the loom is quickly assembled from easily available materials. It is ideal for making short bands, small wall hangings, whimsical dolls, or colorful strips to hang in front of glass doors as warnings. (See Figures C–1, C–2, and C–3 in the color section.)

For a first project designed for young children to make or for you to make for them to play with, you will need four plastic drinking straws, four brightly colored pipe cleaners, 12" long, two small buttons or "wiggle eyes," and a couple of small feathers. You will also need several short lengths of yarn, 30" to 36" long.

Thread each straw with one pipe cleaner, leaving some of the pipe cleaner sticking out of each end. (Figure 4–1.) Twist the pipe cleaners together at the top of the straws; this will be the top of the head of the doll. Select the first length of yarn.

Spread the straws with your fingers and lay one end of the thread alongside and between the two center straws. Hold the end with your fingers. Begin weaving over and under the straws to the outside, turn the yarn and weave across all four straws, weaving over the straw you wove under and under the one you wove over. Continue weaving over and under, alternating straws so that you cover the straws closely to make a solid stripe, about 7 rows wide. The stripes can mark sections of clothing or serve as boundaries for different parts of the doll's body. If the weaving seems loose for the first three or four rows, stop and tighten it up from time to time.

Tuck the end of the weft down in the woven area with a needle or crochet hook, and begin weaving a new weft. When the straws are covered about three-fourths of the way

18

down, slip them down along the pipe cleaners, leaving the weaving on the pipe cleaners. Glue the "wiggle eyes" or sew the small buttons on the top section of the weaving for the face. Twist the remaining pipe cleaners in pairs for legs, add a feather or two, a hat, or a ruffle of cloth for a bonnet and your doll is ready for play.

For the second project, a small wall-hanging band, use yarn instead of pipe cleaners for the warp. (Figure 4–2.) Small dried weeds, bells, beads, or straw flowers may be added to the woven hanging at the end.

You will use six plastic straws and six strands of yarn twice the length needed for the wall hanging plus about six extra inches on each end for fringe and a hanger. You will also need weft yarns, two or three yards in length, of contrasting or closely related colors.

Fold each strand of warp yarn in half. Pull the loop of yarn down through the straw with a crochet hook or a piece of string tied to the loop. Pull the string or crochet hook through the straw so that the loop appears at one end of the straw, and the two loose ends of the warp stick out at the other opening. Take care not to pull the yarns all the way through the straws. Anchor the looped ends to a clipboard or fasten them to a work surface with strong tape to give the loom some tension and to leave your hands free to hold the straws and to weave.

Weaving begins about halfway down the straw. Use one of the weft yarns for a while, then alternate, making wide and narrow stripes. Weave over and under the straws in the same manner as you did in the first straw loom project. Cover the straws firmly. Stop from time to time to pull the weft so that the straws stay close together. When the straws are about three-fourths of the way covered with weaving, slip them down along the warp threads, leaving about one-fourth of their length covered.

Repeat the weft weaving until your wall hanging has reached the desired length. Now slip the straws all the way out and clip the weft end, leaving enough weft for tucking back up into the weaving with a needle or crochet hook to anchor and conceal it. You may anchor the beginning of the weft down in the weaving in the same way. Glue small dried flowers or weeds to the surface or add small shells, cones, or other little treasures you have collected to add decoration or preserve a memory.

Straw-loom bands, which are weft-faced tapestry woven bands, form the exception to the general rule that states that bands are warp-faced.

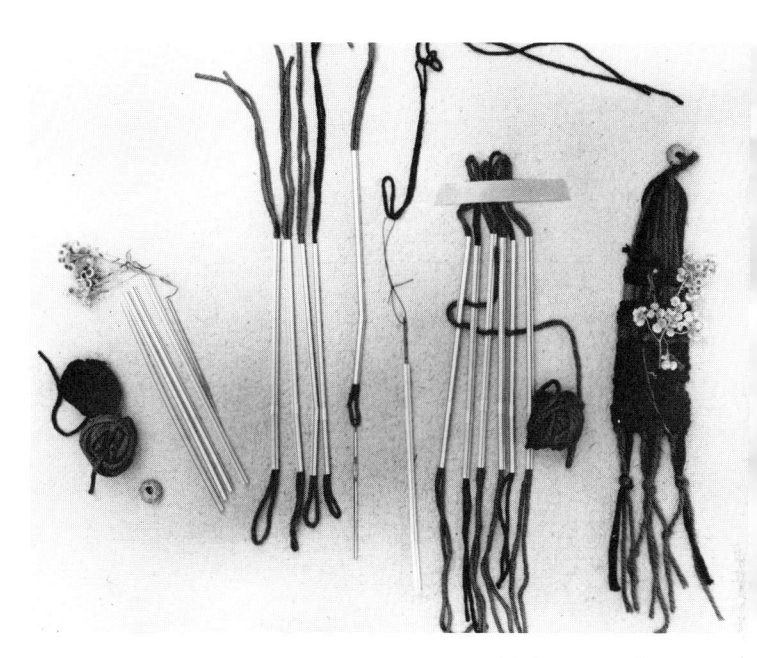

4-2. In the second straw loom project, note: materials for the small wall hanging; how to thread the straws; how to weave; and the finished hanging.

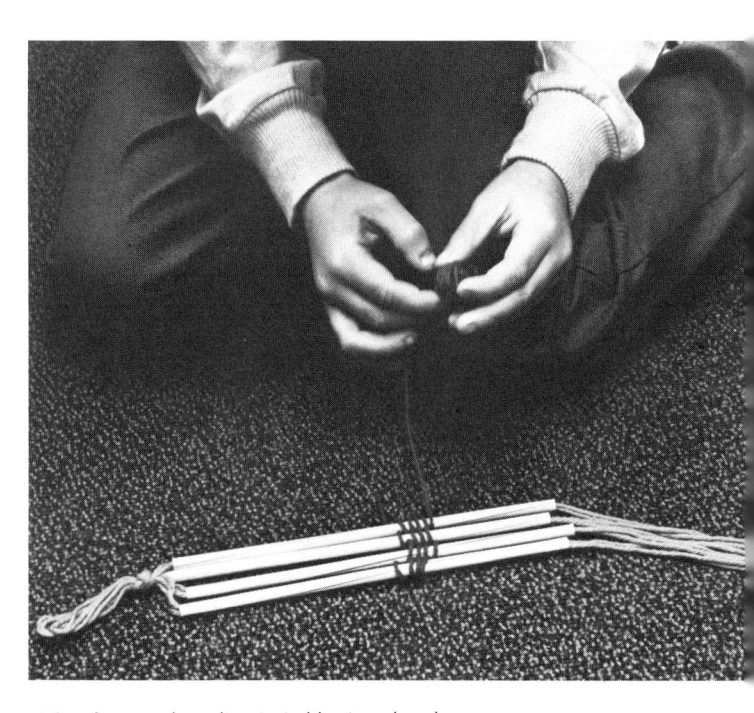

4-3. A second-grader starts his straw band.

19

5.
hungarian-loom bands

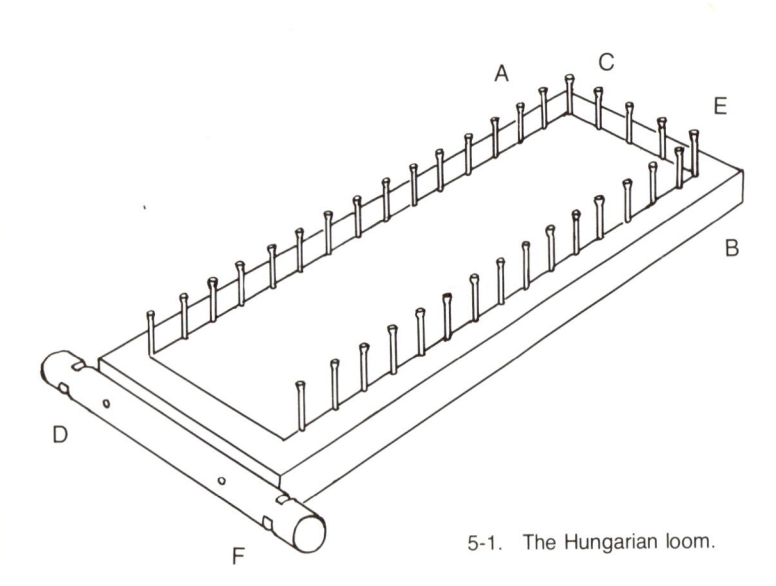

5-1. The Hungarian loom.

The Hungarian band (and also the twined band, which is discussed in the next chapter) can be used as joinings, trimmings, or joined together to make vests, pillows, ponchos, or any other fabric that is of a generally rectangular shape.

The Hungarian band loom, as well as its close relative the twining loom, is easy to make in any number of sizes and from the simplest materials. Figure 5–1 shows the basic plan for the Hungarian loom. Longer or shorter, wider or narrower looms can be built if you need a certain size for a joining or trimming, or if you need a band of a special shape—for example, one that is wider at one end than the other. Almost any weaving yarn is suitable for use with both the Hungarian and twining looms, from fine cotton or wool yarns to heavy rug yarns and jute. Sisal and jute can be used on either the Hungarian or twining loom to make doormats. (Figure 5–2.) The loom can be made to suit the project and the yarn by changing the distance between the nails as well as the overall size. (See Figure C–5 in the color section.)

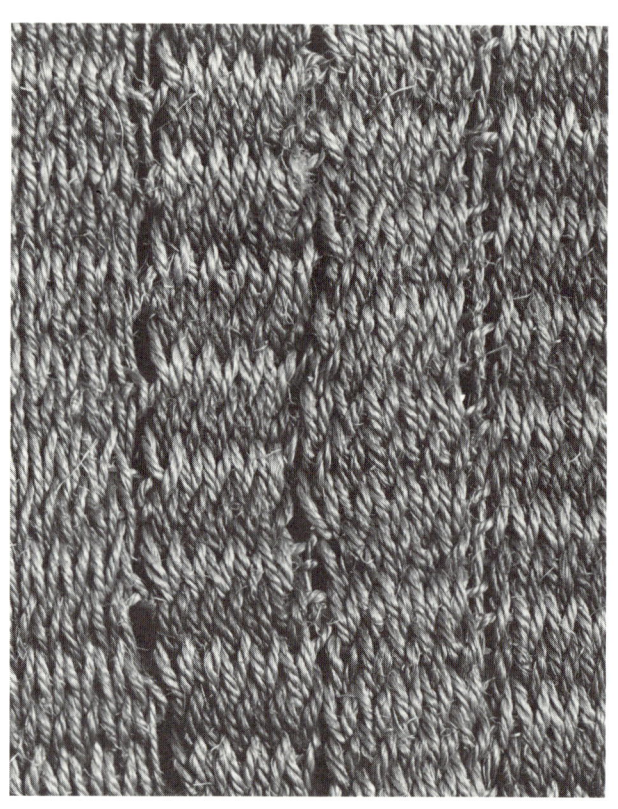

5-2. This jute doormat was made of Hungarian loom woven strips. When you use jute or sisal, wear gloves and keep the material wet while you weave.

To construct the Hungarian loom you will need a handful of 1" headless nails and a piece of ¾" or 1" plywood about 12½" long and 2½" wide, sanded smooth, and about 3½" of small doweling. You will also need a few rubber bands and ten or more bobbins.

On the plywood board draw a pencil line, AB, ½" down from the top, and lines CD and EF the length of the loom about ½" from the edge. Mark the nail holes with a template or pattern about ½" apart along the pencil lines. Note that the nails are not directly across from each other, but are staggered so the tension will be more uniform and a flatter band will be made. If the nails are directly across from each other, the band has a tendency to twist a bit, and the warps will not be even in length.

Drive in the nails in such a way as to leave them ½" above the board. The last five nails are placed across the top of the loom and the short dowel is nailed to the bottom of the loom. Saw a notch in each side of the dowel to hold tension in the weft thread while you weave.

5-3. With the Hungarian loom are shown the rubber bands used to hold the warp yarns in place, a sample of each color of cardboard bobbin, and the five bands that were woven on the loom and joined to make a mat.

You can make your bobbins of cardboard cut 2½" by 1½" with a notch in each end for wrapping the yarns around and a small slit to hold the end of the yarn when you start to wind. (Figure 5–3.) You could also use argyle bobbins. To make

5-4. The warps have been attached to rocks to maintain tension on an ancient loom of possible Greek origin. The loom was set up for demonstration purposes by Alette Skille.

the weaving easier, have half of the bobbins one color and the other half another color. Thus, in your first project, half of your warp threads will be wound on one color and the other half on the other color of bobbin.

The Hungarian band loom is a little like the most ancient warp-weighted looms of the early Greek weavers in that the warp threads are held at the top of the loom and then hang free, controlled and weighted slightly by the bobbins. Other cultures adopted the weighted loom and it is still used in some remote villages in northern Norway.

For the first project — five bands the length of the loom which you can then join together to make a hot-dish mat or a small table mat — you will need the loom, a couple of rubber bands or wire twisters, and one skein each light blue and yellow cotton rug yarn. You will also need ten bobbins, five of a light color and five of a dark color.

If your loom is 12½" long, your five bands will be approximately 12" when finished, excluding fringe. For the first band and all additional bands, cut five strands of light blue cotton yarn about thirty inches long and cut five strands of yellow yarn the same length. Some cotton yarns will shrink in washing, so you could preshrink the yarns before you weave or expect some shrinkage of the finished mat when it is washed.

Double each strand and tie a knot an inch and a half below the folded loop. If you leave an equal amount when you finish weaving, you will have a fringe at each end of the band. Next, wind the free ends of the blue yarn, the ends opposite the knotted end, on the "b" bobbins and the free ends of the yellow yarn on the "a" bobbins, leaving about six inches unwound.

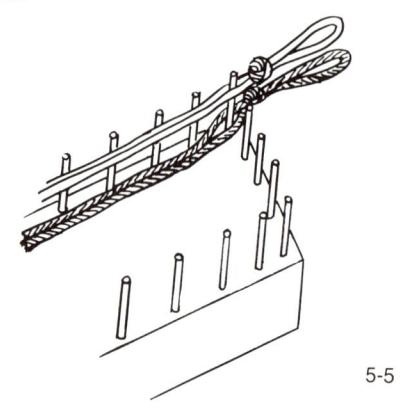

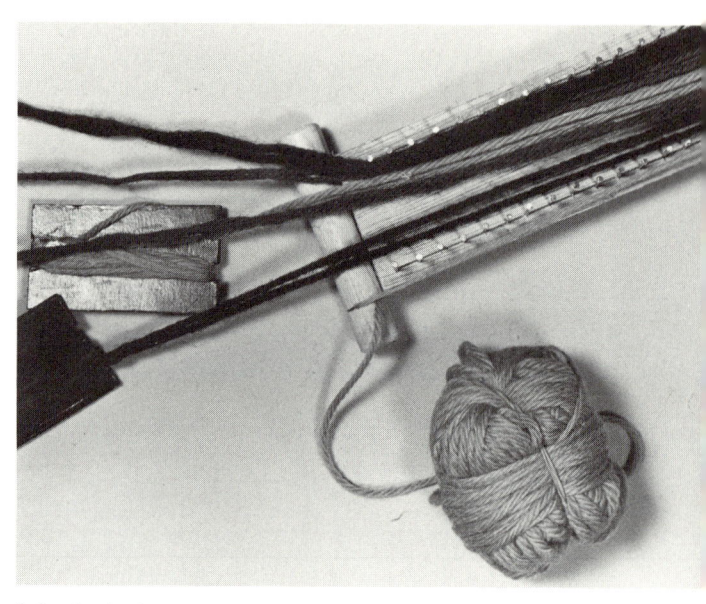

5-6. Anchoring the weft.

5-5

Place the five knots of the blue yarn over the five nails across the top of the loom, one knot to each nail. Then place each one of the yellow knots on top of one of the blue knots. (Figure 5–5.) Hold the warp ends in place across the loom with a rubber band close to the nails.

Any combination of contrasting or closely related colors that you choose will do and after you have woven a few bands you might try placing the warps on the bottom row in a light, dark, light, dark, light sequence and the top row in a dark, light, dark, light, dark sequence. (See Figure 5–15, No. 3, for the resulting pattern.)

To weave, lift all of the light threads, the yellow threads, up and lay them back over the top of the loom and rest them on the work space, being careful not to pull any of them off the nails. The rubber band should hold them on.

Wind one of the cotton rug yarns left from the warp into a ball for weft and fasten the loose or free end to the first nail on the left side of the loom at the top with a knot. Pass the weft thread across the lower warp threads around the first nail on the right side. Pull the weft thread down the side of the loom and wrap it around the small dowel at the base of the loom, slipping it into the notch and giving it another turn or two to hold it firm while you weave. (Figure 5–6.) You may want to keep the ball of weft inside a small plastic bag or drop it into a small container — a bowl or basket — so that it won't roll around while you are weaving.

Figure 5–7 shows you how to change the shed. Pick up the first double thread lying on the loom and pass it between the two strands of the first warp pair in group I so that the two pairs of warp change places, one going through the other. Be *certain* that the exchange is made in the same way throughout the work. The direction of the pattern depends upon the direction of the warp exchanges. If the warp exchanges are wrong, your weaving might look like Figure 5–8. When the exchanges are made correctly, the results look a little like knitting.

For each shed change the weft will be moved across the loom from one nail to the opposite nail, brought down the side of the loom, and anchored in the notch in the dowel. Then

5-7. Changing the shed.

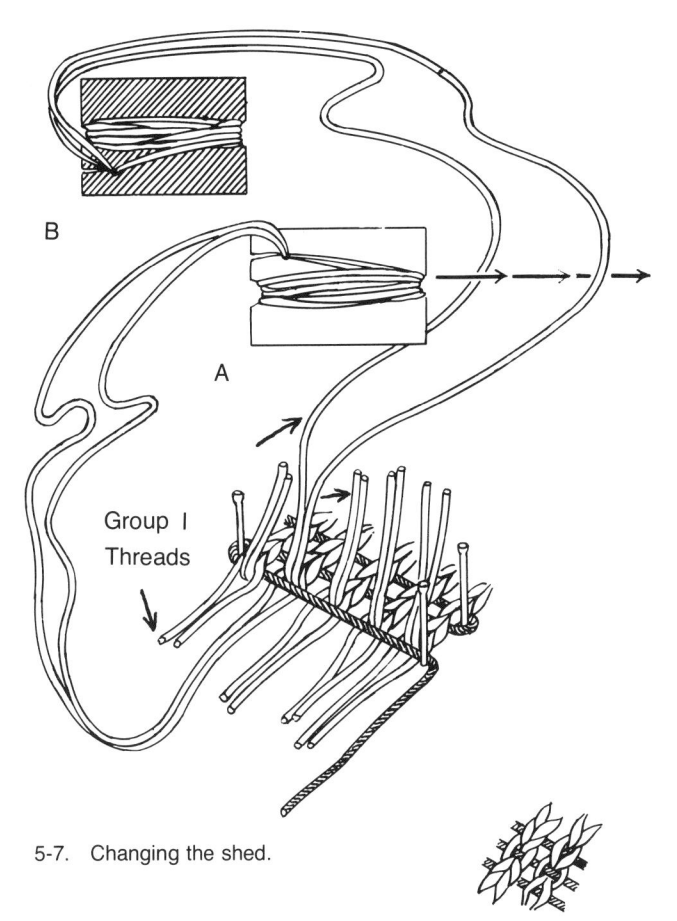

5-8. The results of incorrect warp pair exchanges.

once again you exchange the pairs of warps. If you must leave your work half-finished, place a rubber band around the loom to hold the upper warps in place and another rubber band across the lower pairs to hold them in place, so that the loom may be moved around without the bobbins and the yarns getting all tangled together.

When you have reached the end of the loom, this band will be complete. Cut the weft from the ball of yarn, leaving about five to six inches of yarn to weave back into the band one row at a time for three or four rows. Use a needle or crochet hook to do this weaving. This will take care of the weft and will also secure the weaving, but you might also tie the pairs of warp fringes together with an overhand knot after you have removed the band from the loom. (Figure 5–9.)

When you are ready to take the band off the loom, remove the rubber band from the top end of the loom. Loosen the weft loops on one side by lifting them carefully off the nails,

5-9. An overhand knot.

one at a time. The other side will lift off all the nails at once. Once you have clipped the loops at the top of the band for fringe, your band is finished. Repeat these steps for all five bands.

After you have woven all the bands, press them lightly with a warm iron so that they are flat and straight, but don't pull or twist them. Lay the bands side by side (not overlapping) on a flat surface, and pin only the edges together, first at the ends and then one or two times in between. The bands are reversible, so move them around until you have the weft loops matching up. Try to line the weft-turning loops together side by side or mesh them. Figure 5–10 shows three ways to join the bands. In the first procedure (a) you thread two needles with joining thread that matches either of the warp threads and place the bands side by side with the weft loops touching. The two joining threads cross in between the two loops and then each needle and thread goes through a weft loop and makes the next cross between the loops. In the second method (b), the weft loops are meshed and a single thread does the joining. Don't pull; just keep the sides together and gently join them. If the loops are large, you can use a third method (c), which doesn't require a joining thread. With a crochet hook, you pull a loop first from one side through a loop directly opposite in the other band. Then with this loop

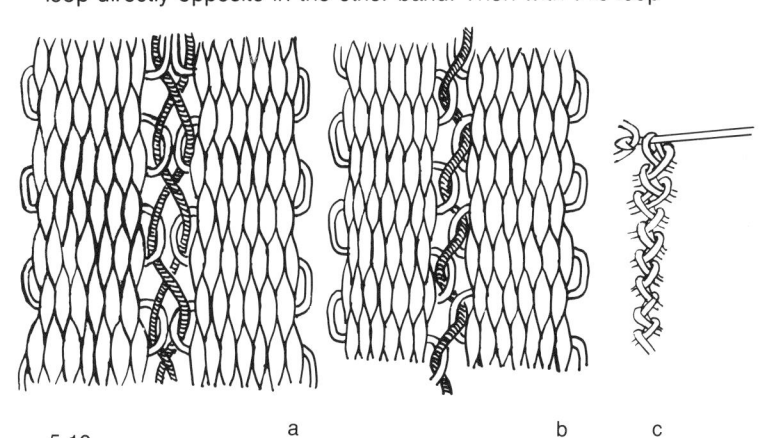

5-10.   a   b   c

23

on the hook, pull the next loop from the opposite side through the loop on the hook. Place a thread through the last loop in such a way as to keep it from unraveling. A tag end of weft at the top of one band can be used. The general rule to remember is always to join weft to weft, not warp to warp or warp to weft; otherwise you will weaken the structure.

A single band can be used in a narrow wall space as holiday decoration or on a door. Holly berries, bells, dried flowers and weeds, or small art objects can be glued or sewn on after the band has been woven. Chenille, gold rickrack, and rug wool were used for the band in Figure 5–11, but many other yarns could be combined. Gold or silver cord, gift ribbon, novelty yarns, jute, nubby cottons, wools or linens, or small embroidered trimming could be woven along with smooth satin cord or worsted wools and mohairs.

To weave the band shown, you will need a loom three inches wide and twelve inches long, with the nails set three-fourths of an inch apart. (You may vary these measurements if you like.) Cut four strands of medium green rug wool eighty inches long, and four strands of chenille, medium green, of the same length. For the center row use an eighty-inch strand of light green chenille and an equal length of gold and white rickrack. Boucle or loop mohair are good substitutes for chenille.

Loop the yarns in pairs (one chenille with one rug wool and chenille with rickrack) over the ring. (Figure 5–12.) Place the ring over the nails at the top of the loom and slip the rubber band over the yarns, holding them close to the nails. Wrap the strands of wool and rickrack around the light set of bobbins and the chenille around the dark set of bobbins.

Lift all of the light set of bobbins and yarn up and lay them back over the top of the loom and the ring and rest them on the work space. Use the green wool rug yarn for weft. Start the weft by tying the starting end to the first nail at the top of the left-hand side of the loom just as you did for the short bands in the first project. Then weave in the same manner as described for the first project until you approach the end of the loom.

Now stop and separate both halves of the weaving from each other with rubber bands or wire twisters. Remove the rubber band from the top of the loom and loosen the loops from one side, carefully lifting them one by one; those on the other side of the loom should lift off all at once. Lift the ring off the nails and move the weaving up and off the loom. Replace about two inches of the woven band carefully over the first few nails, keeping the weft loops in the correct order. (Figure 5–13.)

5-11

5-12. Hook the ring over the two nails to give tension to the weaving.

Lay in the weft, remove the twisters or rubber bands from the two halves of the warp, and continue weaving until you need to move the band up again. If your loom is longer, you will have to move up only once, but the shorter-length loom is more portable and takes up less storage space. If you run out of weft, you can lay in a new one along with the old one for a few shots, as described in Chapter 2. To finish the band, cut off the weft, leaving a tag end to weave back up into the band. Add decorative touches and your wall hanging is complete.

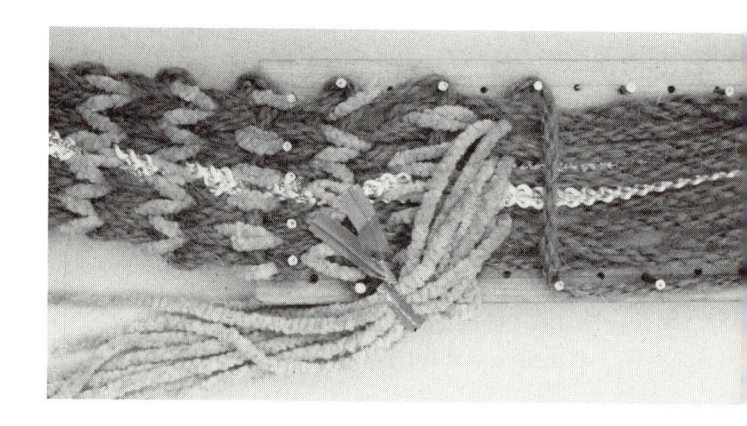

5-13. The band has been moved up so the weaving can continue.

24

You should plan ahead if you want to make a color change or add warp, because you will then be using the looped ends of the warp pairs. In such a procedure, you leave the looped end of the warp threads free and wind this end around the bobbin. You tie the other cut ends in a knot, leaving a fringe if you wish, and place them around the starter nails at the top of the loom. (Figure 5–14.)

5-14

When your weaving has brought you to the end of the bobbin, take a new warp thread and double it. Slip one end through the loop on the old warp thread, pull it out even with the other end of the new warp thread, and wind the ends on the bobbin. In this simple way, you will have made a smooth joining. You can do this only once per weaving, because if you use the looped ends to loop through each other, then you will have two free ends at each end of the warp. To tie free ends in a knot would make a large lump in the weaving that would show.

Figure 5–16 shows some additional patterns that you can try on your Hungarian loom. The top row of squares represents the first row of warps that are placed over the nails, and the second row represents the group of warps that you place on top of the first group. Figure 5–15 shows what the patterns will look like in your finished bands.

Hungarian weaving is a kind of warp twining, because as the two pairs of warp yarns exchange they encircle the weft. Another possibility, however, is *weft* twining, which is a method of using a pair of weft threads to encircle a warp thread or pair of threads. Although the Hungarian band loom (for warp twining) and the twining loom (for weft twining) resemble each other, the woven results can be very different. The Hungarian loom produces only one pattern with the weaving, while there are many ways in which weft twining can be made to produce different designs, one of which duplicates the small chevron pattern of the Hungarian weaving.

Weaving on the Hungarian loom can be simple and relatively fast. It can be done by two children, two adults, or an adult and child, as well as by one person alone. (Figure 5–17.) Weaving on the twiner can be more complex and is a one-person process. Although the twining loom is similar to the Hungarian loom, we will discuss weaving on the twiner in a separate chapter, since there will be different techniques involved.

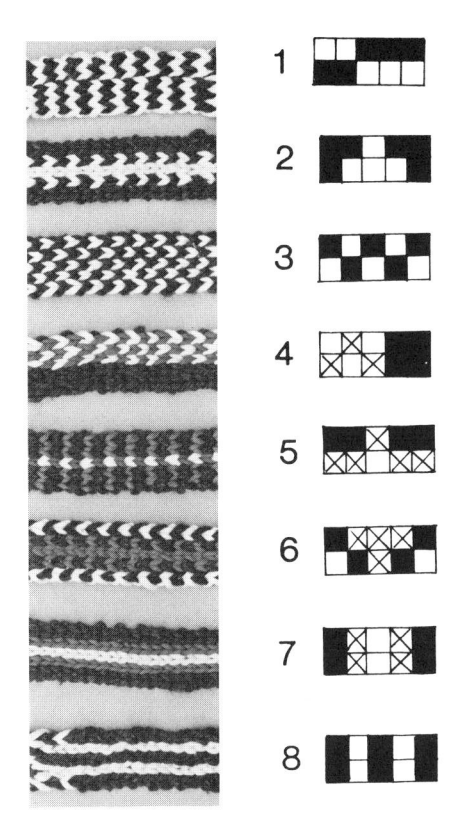

5-15. *Left:* Eight different kinds of patterns for Hungarian-loom bands.

5-16. *Right:* The pattern drafts for the bands in Figure 5–15.

5-17. In this Hungarian weaving for two, Gina and Ric Griffin are the weavers.

6.
twining-loom bands

The uses of the bands made on the twining loom are very similar to the uses for the Hungarian bands, as discussed earlier. (See page 20.) In addition to these, if you weave with heavy wool, the twining loom can also be used to make rug strips to be joined together for area rugs.

There are many good sources for information about classical twining as done by the Indian people in prehistoric times. The "Basketmakers" mentioned earlier used twining techniques in making blankets of rabbit skin and the Navajos, too, may have been twiners. Even today the Salish Indians of the Pacific Northwest use twining to construct their thick, compact blankets. (For more history, one good source is *Weft Twining* by Virginia Harvey and Harriet Tidball.)

The weaving method on the twining loom is a simplification of true twining. The results are the same as in classic twining, but only one strand at a time is woven instead of the traditional pairs, and a needle is used as a shuttle or yarn carrier rather than the fingers. The weaving satisfies the general definition of twining as the act of turning two or more yarns around each other so as to enclose other yarns.

Weaving on the twiner can be set close together; more yarns can be woven and packed in the space, giving a greater variety of colors and designs than can be obtained on the Hungarian loom. For easy weaving on the Hungarian loom you can manipulate a maximum of seven pairs of warp, but twenty weft pairs can easily be used in twining with approximately the same-width loom.

To build the loom, use a board 1″ thick and 2″ wide by 12″ long, and two ¼″ dowels 12″ long. You will also need forty to fifty 1-17 wire brads or two-penny finishing nails, a No. 13 tapestry needle, and a short length of ½″ dowel, about 1½″ to 2″ long. (Figure 6–1.)

Hold the ¼″ dowel on the top edge of the board with rubber bands and mark the nail holes ¾″ apart along the dowel. As in the Hungarian loom, the nail holes should be staggered,

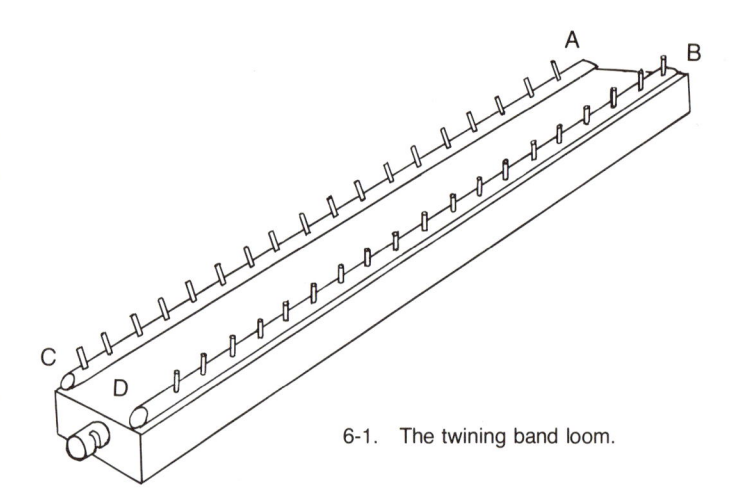

6-1. The twining band loom.

and not directly across from each other, in order to give an even length to each warp. If you have a small drill, you should drill the nail holes first so you won't split the dowel. Next, drive the nails into the dowel so as to leave approximately ½″ extending above the loom.

Place the short dowel in the center of the end of the loom. Drill a hole and set the dowel in. Saw two notches in the dowel close to the loom to hold the warp taut while you weave.

The width of the loom determines the width of the band. Because weaving is moved up in the same manner as on the Hungarian loom, the twiner need only be as long as it is convenient for you to use.

The first band you try to weave could be made of washable yarns and used as trim to turn a plain baby blanket into a personal gift. (Figures 6–2 and 6–3.) With a longer band, you could trim a full-sized blanket.

Use two colors of acrylic boucle or other washable baby yarns for the weft and a smooth acrylic yarn for the warp. Cut 24 strands of the light-color—white was used for the band shown in Figure 6–3—and 24 strands of the dark yarn, blue, 44″ long, for a finished band of 38″.

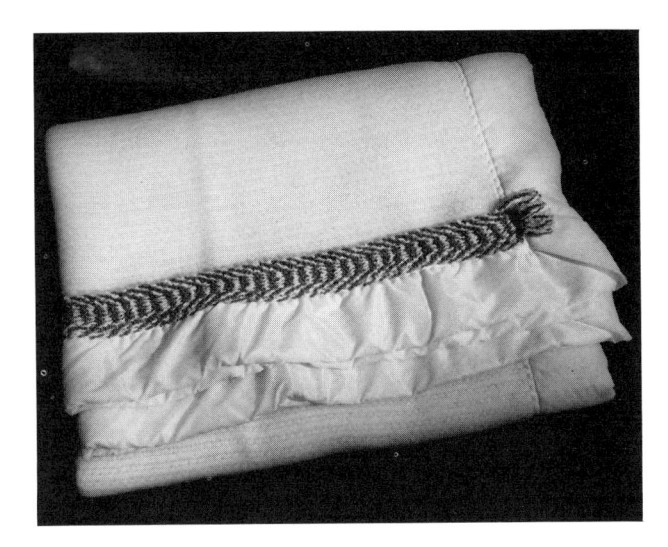

6-2. A baby blanket trimmed with a twined band.

6-3. A detail of the twined band shown in Figure 6-2.

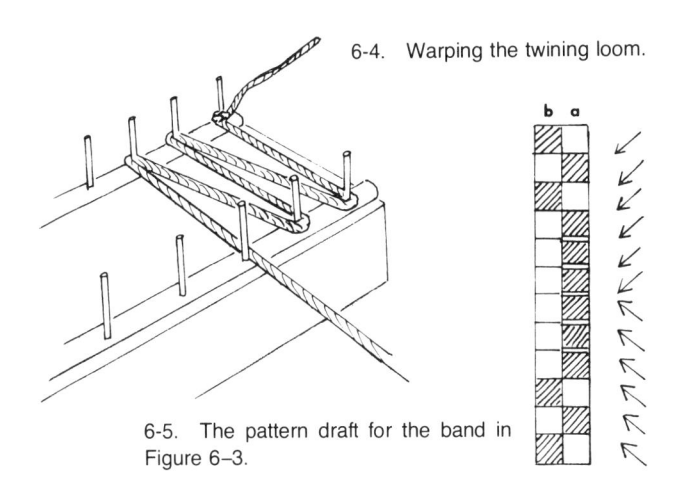

6-4. Warping the twining loom.

6-5. The pattern draft for the band in Figure 6-3.

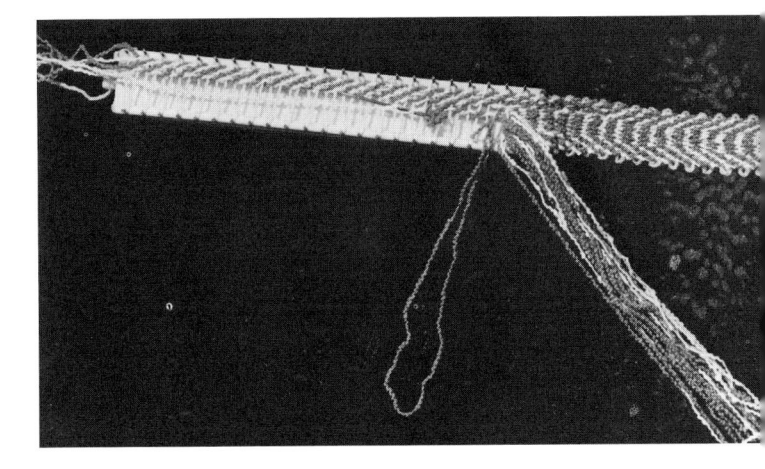

6-6. The twined band in progress is shown.

Wind the smooth, light-color acrylic yarn in a ball for warp, and tie the warp end to the top nail, leaving an end of about 5" to weave back in to lock the end rows. Wind the warp zigzag across the loom (Figure 6-4), nail to nail to the end of the loom, where you then wind it around the dowel, down in the notch so that it is held while you weave.

Thread your tapestry needle with the first white thread, which we will call the "a" thread. Weave this thread *under* and over the warps for the length of the loom, leaving about 2" at the beginning for fringe. Next, thread your needle with one strand of the blue, which will be the "b" thread. Study the direction of the "b" thread in Figure 6-5; the arrows show the direction the needle will take over the first warp. (See the instructions for reading the pattern drafts on page 31.) The white yarn has gone *under* the first warp.

Start the second blue strand *under* and over the warps, following the path of the first white strand. The white thread of this second pair will take the same path that the first blue strand took, crossing the blue weft and encircling and covering the warp. The third pair of wefts will repeat the pathway of the first pair.

The middle section of the band uses six pairs of weft yarns, and the last three pairs of wefts complete the band by making a reverse diagonal. When the width of the loom has been twined, lift the band off and move it up to continue.

Lift up each warp loop, one at a time, from one side of the loom and then carefully lift off the loops from the other side. Loosen the warp from the notch in the dowel. Then place some of the woven band back on the nails, relocating about three warp loops on each side, at the AB end of the loom (see Figure 6-1), and commence winding the warp once more, back and forth from nail to nail down the loom.

Repeat the weaving as before until the weft yarns have all been twined. Now cut off the warp, leaving an end of 5" to be woven back up in the band. Remove the band and weave the two warp ends back into the band, using the needle to insert the warp across the rows. You can attach the band to the blanket by hand sewing just below the satin binding. If you machine stitch the ends of the band, it will be more durable for washing, or you can remove the band when you wash the blanket.

6-7. The tenth band of the area rug is being joined to the other nine.

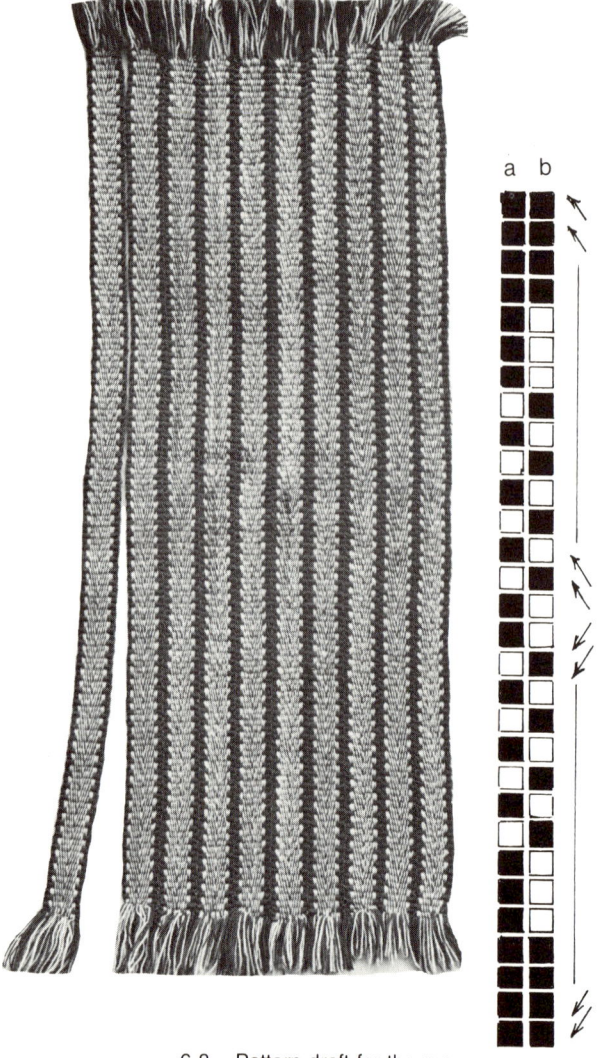

6-8. Pattern draft for the rug.

The rug in Figure 6–7 was made of brown and yellow-green rug wool, with a rust-colored warp. We joined ten bands, 53" long excluding fringe and 2½" wide, to make this area rug. For a rug like this the loom should consist of a 1" x 3" board, 28" long and with the nails set ¾" apart.

The first pairs of weft are brown and are twined compactly as shown in Figure 6–8. The next three pairs are brown and yellow and are also twined compactly. The next 16 pairs are brown and yellow-green and the last seven pairs are the same as the first seven.

When the bands are finished, join them warp loop to warp loop with a yarn that matches the warp. (See Figure 5–10.) To finish the fringe you could knot the ends in pairs or you can give a flat finish to the fringe as is shown in Figure 6–9. Thread one fringe through the eye of a needle, then push the needle and the fringe end squarely through the opposite fringe, keeping the needle and the fringe end close to the top of the fringe you are threading.

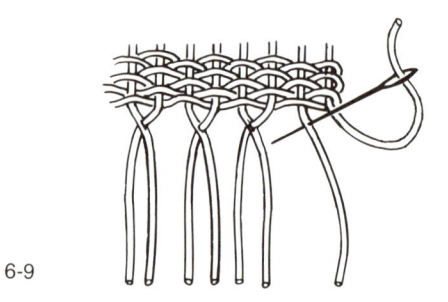

6-9

To make the ruana shown in Figure 6–10, you need two rectangular pieces of hand-woven or machine-woven fabric 50" long and 19" wide, excluding fringe. (Figure 6–11.) The four bands to be used for joining and trimming can be made on any band loom. Since the ruana-style garment in Figure 6–10 was made of handwoven fabric composed of mohair, alpaca, and handspun yarns, soft bands of the same yarns were used. A band woven on the Hungarian loom or twined on the twining loom will be of a soft, loose construction if you use lofty or loosely spun yarns. If the garment is made of commercially woven fabric or a firmer handwoven fabric, you might want to use the inkle loom to weave the bands. (See Chapter 8.)

The two center bands are joined to each other about two-thirds of the distance up the back. They are then attached to the garment the full length of its two sides, and the edging bands are also attached to the full length of the outside of the two rectangles.

6-10. Twined bands trim a ruana-style garment and are joined halfway up the back.

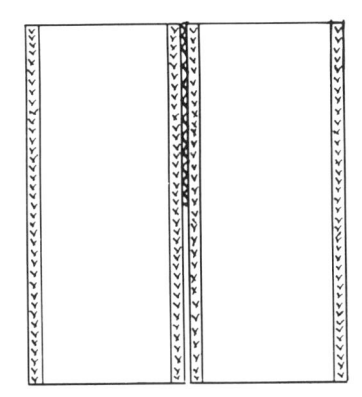

6-11. A general pattern for the rectangular ruana.

Another garment made of two rectangles is the quechquemitl shown in Figure 6–12, which required sixteen woven bands. Eight were Hungarian loom bands and the other eight were woven on the twining loom, using pattern number 2 in Figure 6–16, which creates the small chevron that so closely resembles Hungarian band weaving. You may use rugged, nubby, or soft yarns for this poncholike garment. We used alpaca and brushed mohair and kept the design simple and unobtrusive so that the texture of the yarns could dominate. Figure 6–13 shows the general pattern for making a quechquemitl. The two rectangles are joined together to make the three-cornered garment by first attaching the end of one rectangle to one-half of the side of the other. Then end AB is attached to one half of the side of the other rectangle, as indicated by the arrows.

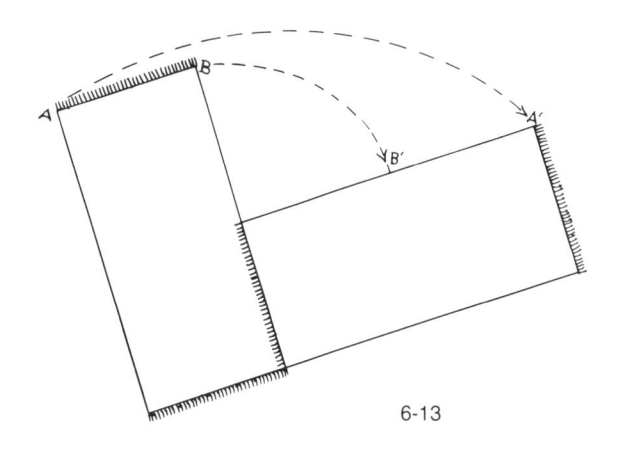

6-12. A quechquemitl composed of Hungarian loom and twined loom bands.

6-13

6-14. A twining band pillow in progress.

The small pillow in Figure 6-14 was made of bands with various combinations of twining "stitches"; you will no doubt think of countless other applications for woven bands. Anything of a generally rectangular shape can be made of bands

6-15. The basic twining stitches.

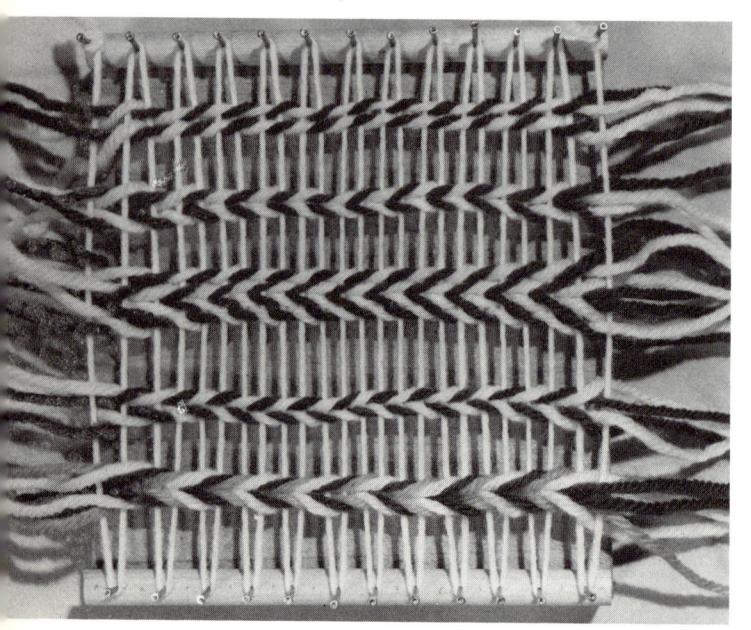

or be trimmed with or joined by bands. You can make a bedspread, rug, curtain, room divider, table covering, wall hanging, tapestry, pillow, shirt, skirt, vest, afghan, stole, or wind chimes, to name but some of the objects that come to mind.

The method of writing the pattern drafts for the twined bands had to be invented because the loom and the idea of twined bands was new to us, even though twining is probably one of the most ancient weaving techniques. When we examined the Hungarian loom closely and the path of the weft as it moves from nail to nail, we realized that the weft path could become a warp path and that more variety could be achieved by using weft twining techniques to produce another style of woven band. We had to decide on some way of indicating the pattern directions for these woven bands, and we hope these drafts will be clear and easy for you to follow. As always in this book, our instructions are meant to be elementary starting points, and we hope you will improve

6-16. The patterns in Figure 6-15 are created with these techniques.

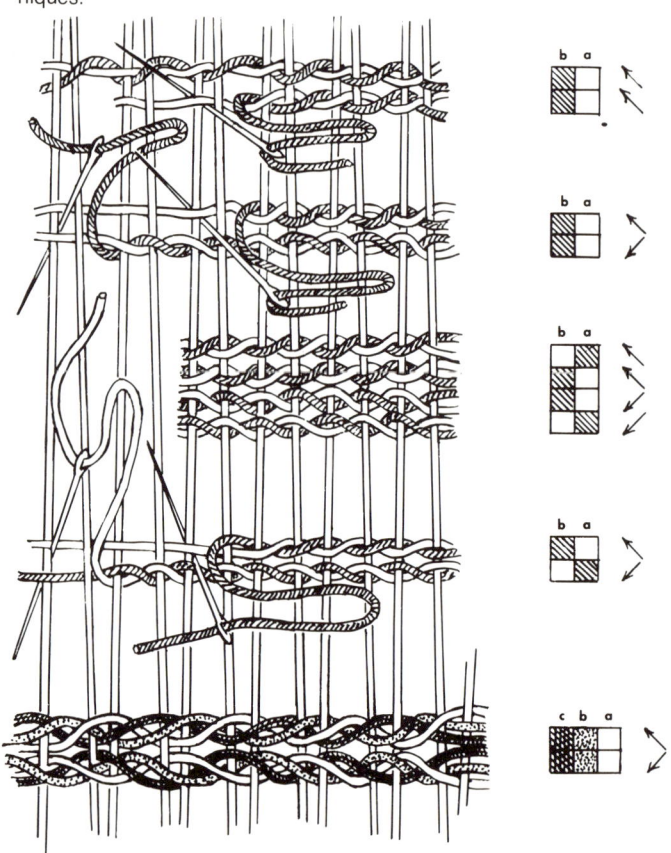

6-17. The basic patterns in Figures 6–15 and 6–16 yield designs like these.

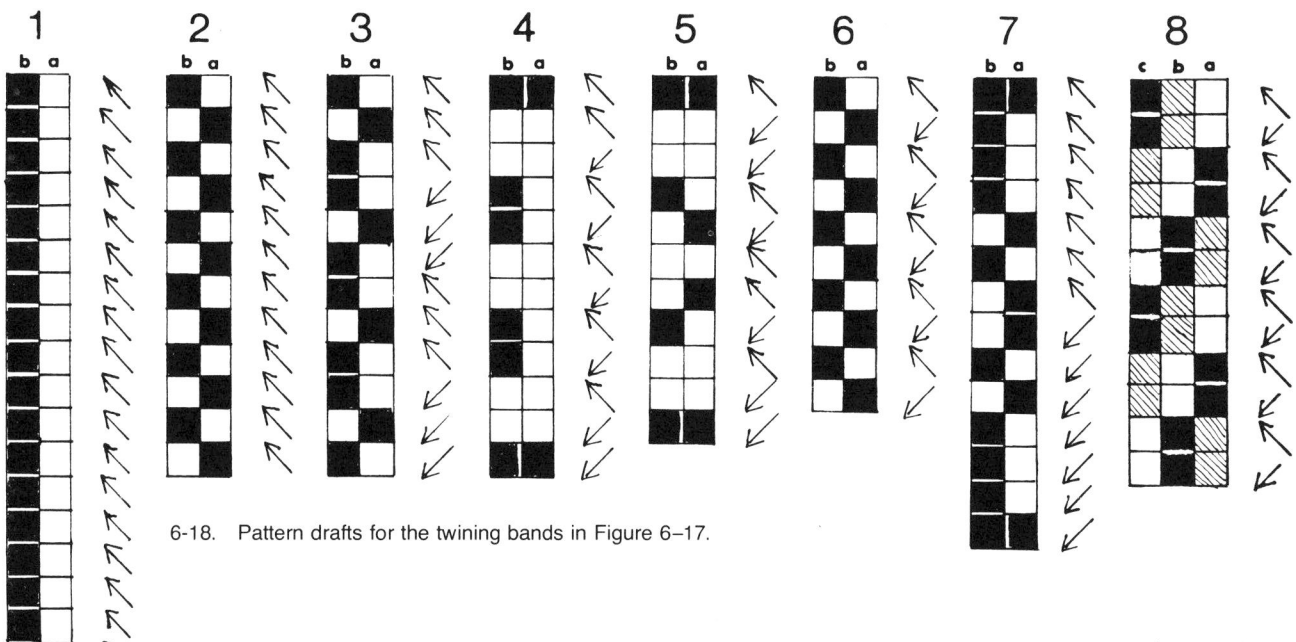

6-18. Pattern drafts for the twining bands in Figure 6–17.

upon them or change them to suit your own ways of weaving.

The pattern blocks should be read in pairs, just as you weave in pairs. The top two blocks represent the first pair of wefts. The right-hand or "a" block is the first yarn to be woven; it starts *under* the first warp and continues on its over-and-under straight path. The left-hand or "b" block is the twiner weft; the arrow to the right of the blocks indicates the direction the needle should take as it twines along the "a" threads, enclosing a warp each time. Figure 6–16, which illustrates the basic twining patterns, also demonstrates what is meant by "the direction of the needle." Look at Figure 6–17 to see how these patterns can be combined for a variety of band designs. Band number 1 in Figure 6–17 is an expansion of the pattern shown in the first diagram in Figure 6–16 (this kind of twining is called "compact" twining because it is so closely packed); band number 4 is an expansion of the second diagram; band number 3 and the center of band number 7 use the reverse diagonal shown in the third diagram; band numbers 5 and 6 use the basic stitches shown in the fourth diagram—number 5 uses only two lines of the pattern while number 6 uses the pattern in an overall design; band number 2 uses the first half of the diagonal line of the third diagram in an expanded form; and band number 8 is the three-color pattern depicted in the fifth diagram. Figure 6–18 has the corresponding draft patterns for Figure 6–17.

31

7. rigid-heddle bands

7-1. A variety of heddles.

Even if you are constantly on the move or your home is shrinking to small-apartment size, don't give up weaving. The backstrap loom used with a rigid heddle can give you hours of weaving pleasure. Rigid heddles can be made or purchased from loom supply shops, and can range in size from 5" to 8" high and 5" to 14" wide. They are excellent band weaving looms, but can also be used for weaving strips of fabric, table runners, wall hangings, curtains, or tapestries.

Figure 7–1 shows some rigid heddles, semi-rigid heddles, and a tie bar. To make the rigid heddle at the upper left, you would need woodworking tools, a drill, and some method of holding the dowels in position while the base and top are glued on and while the holes are being drilled. The rigid heddle at the upper right was made from coffee stirrers, with extra string heddles that were attached to increase the number of threads per inch. At the bottom of Figure 7–1 note

C-1. These soda straw weavings were done by pupils of the Ardmore Elementary school under the direction of student instructors of ten or eleven years of age.

C-2. Pat Lanning, an art teacher, made this pipe cleaner doll.

C-3. These soda straw weavings were done by children from ages four to ten.

C-4. Children from ages four to ten wove these inkle and popstick loom bands.

C-5. *At right:* It took only a handful of nails and a small board to make the loom for this loop-wool wall hanging designed and woven by Lucy Mathews with joined and free-hanging Hungarian loom bands.

C-6. These simple inkle patterns are enhanced by the use of well-planned color combinations. (Woven by Priscilla Chong.)

C-7. Tapering rigid heddle bands of subtle colors were joined to make a long skirt. When in fashion, a tapered band like this makes a beautiful necktie.

C-8. Two rigid heddle bands (inkle bands work as well) are joined weft to weft in an enclosed spiral to form a shoulder bag.

C-9. This double-faced band was woven with two rigid heddles, thus making a fabric with two different surface designs. The top surface of the band is at the bottom and the reverse view on top.

C-10. Virginia Joy wove the inkle band specifically for the handwoven afghan.

C-11. The weft float technique as applied to a wide inkle-band scarf. (Priscilla Chong, weaver.)

35

C-12. This woven-band wall hanging demonstrates the importance of the support as a significant part of the hanging. (Woven by Nancy Gano.)

C-13. These vibrant bands were card-woven with soft handspun yarns in warm colors. (Woven by Herbi Gray.)

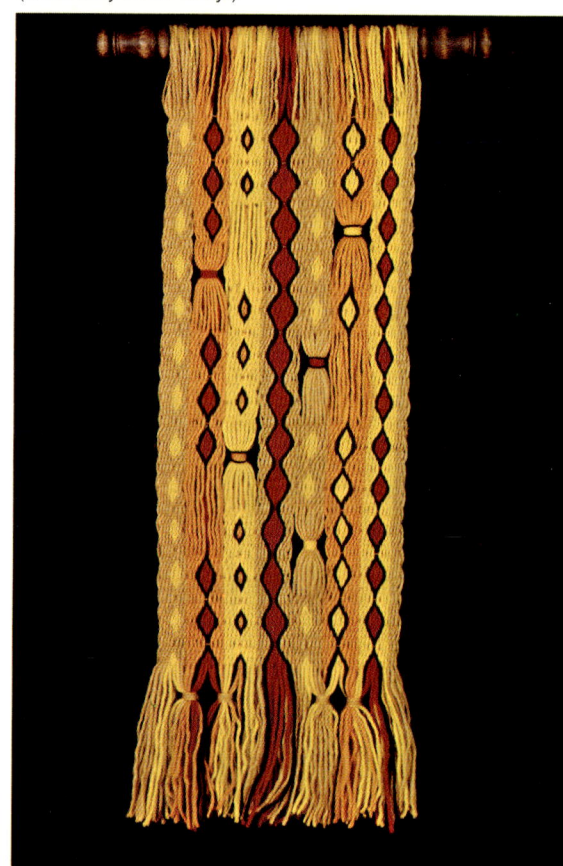

C-14. Card woven bands join four sections of a hand-woven quilt, an excellent way to expand your weaving when your vision is wider than your loom. (Woven by Karen Kaufman.)

C-15. *At left:* Handspun natural wools and subtle card-woven patterns blend together in a magnificent wall hanging woven by Barbara Cade.

C-16. *Below:* A close-up detail of Figure C-15 shows some of the patterns.

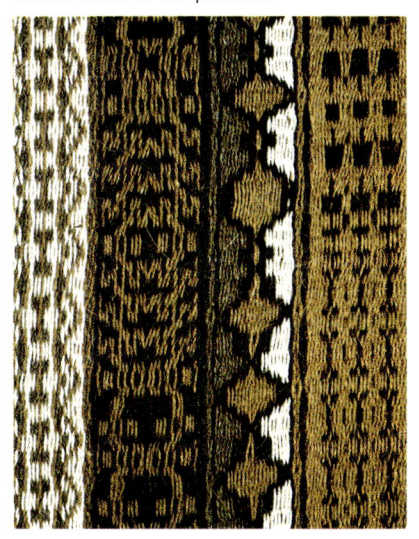

C-18. A single piece of card weaving creates a striking wall hanging. (Woven by Phoebe McAfee.)

C-17. Skillful blending of colors contributes to the originality of the design of these card-woven bands designed and woven by Herbi Gray. The threading drafts for the bands are in Figure 9–28.

37

C-19. Slits and unwoven and wrapped warps add effective design elements to bands planned for sculpture or wall hangings.

C-20. A wide variety of design is achieved through color, weft variations, and easy pick-up patterns.

C-21. Two color blendings from nature's art museum.

38

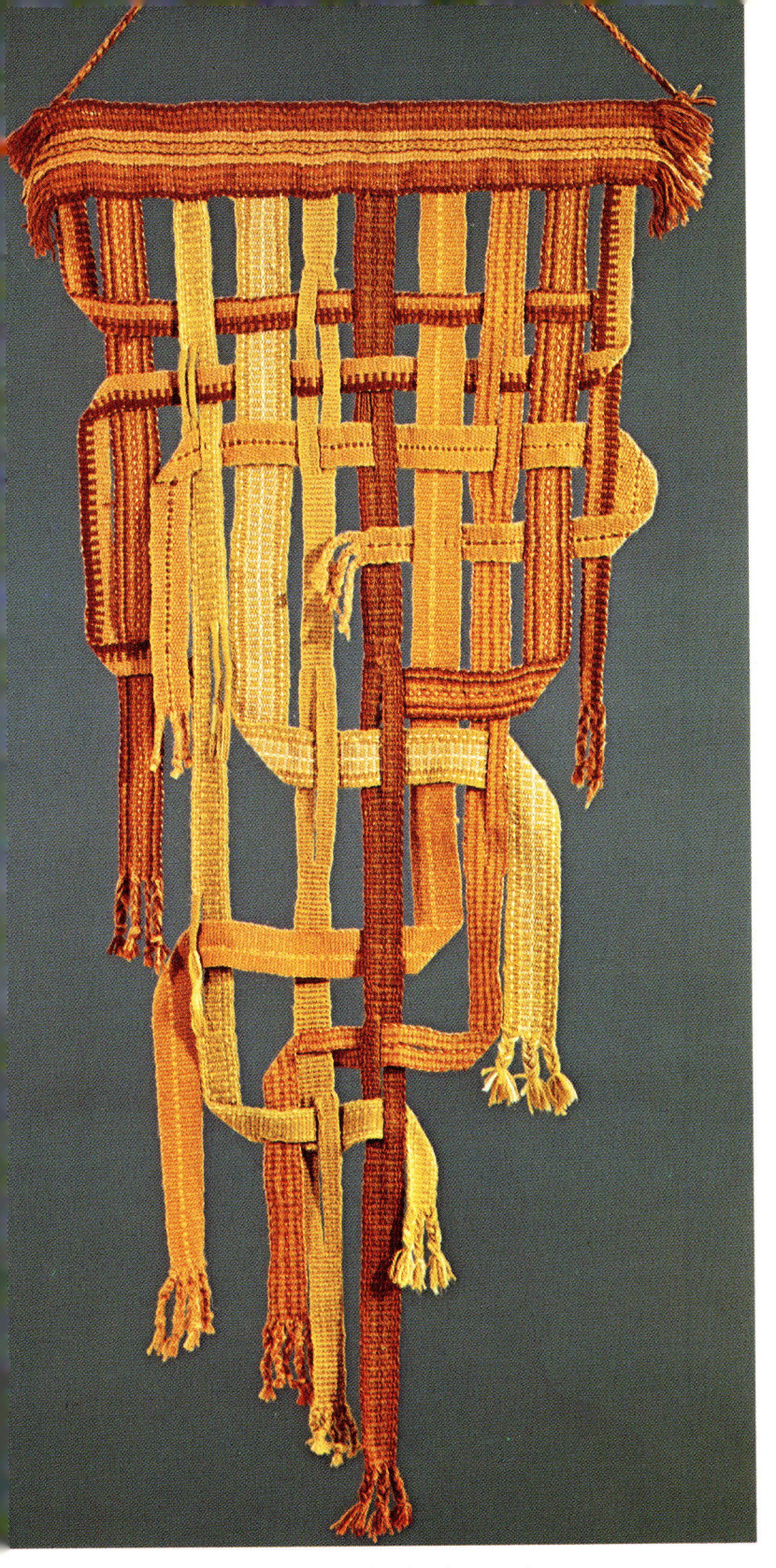

C-22. Woven bands need not be functional, as can be seen from this hanging, which is called "Freeway Interchange."

C-23. A collection of pillows made from a variety of bands: at upper right, a pillow made with inkle-band leftovers and a carrying strap; upper left, a pillow made of twined bands; lower right, another inkle-band pillow made of stuffed bands; lower left, a pillow trimmed with a twined band; and the bottom left, a pillow trimmed with a twined band under another pillow made with band leftovers.

C-24. *Below:* This bedspread (a section of which is shown) is made of sixty-nine joined heddle-woven bands, with a variety of designs and a dominant color.

C-26. A single rigid heddle band with a long slit becomes a novel necklace.

C-25. Small inkle bands were joined to make a colorful pillow; fringes add a tactile and whimsical touch. (Woven by Priscilla Chong.)

C-27. Rigid heddle bands cover seams and serve as decoration for a king-size bedspread.

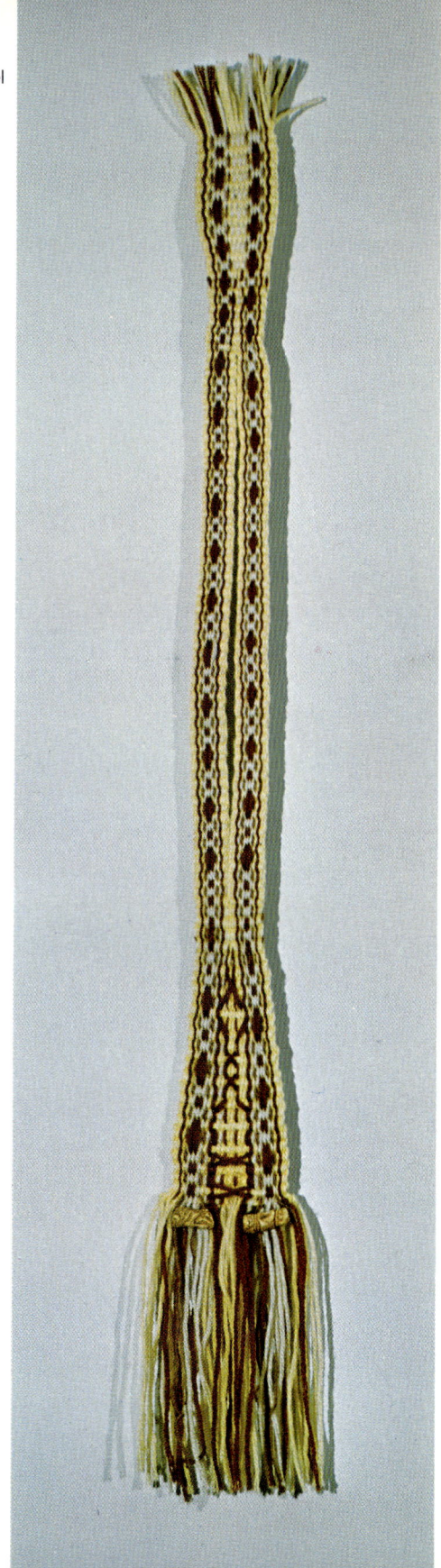

7-2. (Courtesy of Fred and Leslie Hart.)

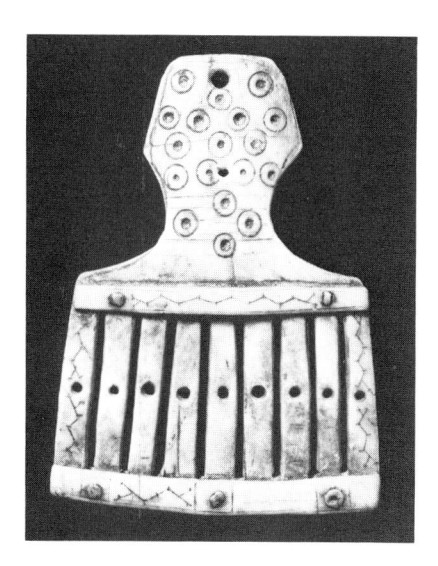

7-3. This Lappish rigid heddle is made of reindeer horn. (From the Norsk Folkemuseum, Oslo, Norway.)

the pop-stick or coffee–stirrer loom which needs no special tools to construct it; in the middle, string heddles fastened to a frame; and at right, the tie bar which is to be used with the frame in Figure 7–18. The detail of a Mexican backstrap rigid heddle in Figure 7–2 shows how auxiliary string heddles increase threads per inch in the border area.

Studies of primitive looms show that early rigid heddles in Europe and Indonesia were carved from one piece of wood. In the eighteenth and nineteenth centuries, English ladies wove on a ribbon loom with the heddle fixed at one end of a box. The warp passing through the slots was raised and lowered to make the sheds. The Lapp women's first belt looms were made of parallel slats of bone, with holes drilled in the center of each one, which were fastened to two larger bone strips at the top and bottom. For nomadic people this device was perhaps more dependable and less bulky than the sets of wooden or bone tablets.(Figure 7–3.) A free translation of the Swedish word for an early rigid heddle, "*bandgrind*," is "band gate," a correspondence we can recognize; a discarded wooden slotted spoon that had outgrown its usefulness in the kitchen might have been the inspiration for this shed-forming device. In order to weave their rough nonfilament strips, the Ainu of Northern Japan constructed a crude warp spacer to be used with an auxiliary heddle. According to Henry Ling Roth in *Studies in Primitive Looms*, this object seems to have been made of a single flat piece of wood perforated at the top and bottom edges with holes large enough to accommodate bundles of warp threads.

In its earliest use the rigid heddle was a part of a backstrap system of weaving and cultures still use this form for weaving both bands and fabric strips, expecially in the warmer countries Africa, South America, and Mexico, where it is comfortable to weave outdoors with the loom hitched to a tree. In the United States today little campers and schoolchildren use simple pop-stick looms, which they hitch up to a table leg or a tree, backstrap style, and weave away on their jean belts and headbands. This arrangement is suitable for a bed patient — the foot of the bed is an ideal hitching post — and even

7-4. A new tactile experience is in store for Janice Ray, who is using a primitive backstrap loom hitched up to a window latch.

the most sophisticated weavers and craftsmen find weaving on this loom a useful addition to their craft.

The rigid heddle is a single unit consisting of slots and holes, an arrangement which separates the two layers of warp threads in an alternating sequence so that every other thread is raised up from every other thread, forming an opening or shed for the filling material or weft. If it is yarn, the weft material should be wound around a shuttle to make weaving easy. You can introduce other weft materials such as bamboo, unspun wools, or whatever else you wish for wall hangings or novelty weaving. (See Chapter 10.)

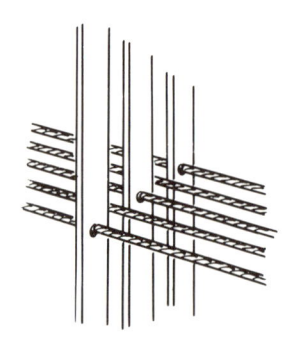

7-5. When you thread a rigid heddle, place the warps in the holes and slots from one side of the loom to the other.

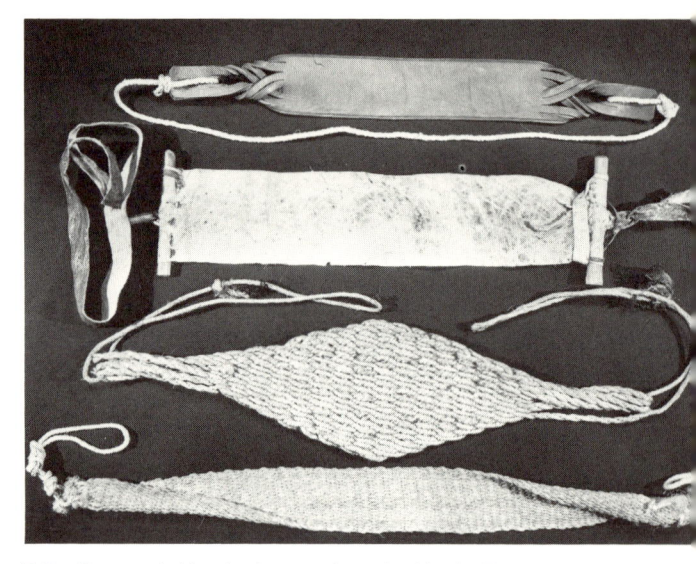

7-7. Some primitive backstraps from the Harriet Tidball collection. (Property of the Costume and Textile Study Center, School of Home Economics, University of Washington.)

The elements of the backstrap loom consist of some kind of rigid heddle, a stationary post to which one end of the warp threads is attached, a cord or strap to go around the weaver's waist, and a dowel or its equivalent to which each end of the waist strap is fastened. This dowel is called a "cloth dowel" because the woven fabric is fastened to it. Since the weaver is the tensioning device for this type of weaving, she is also part of the loom. In the simple backstrap loom shown in Figure 7–8, two curtain rings taped to a wooden hanger serve as the cloth stick. Drilled popsicle sticks were laced to two small flat boards (tongue depressors can be used), and a backstrap of twisted cord completes the loom.

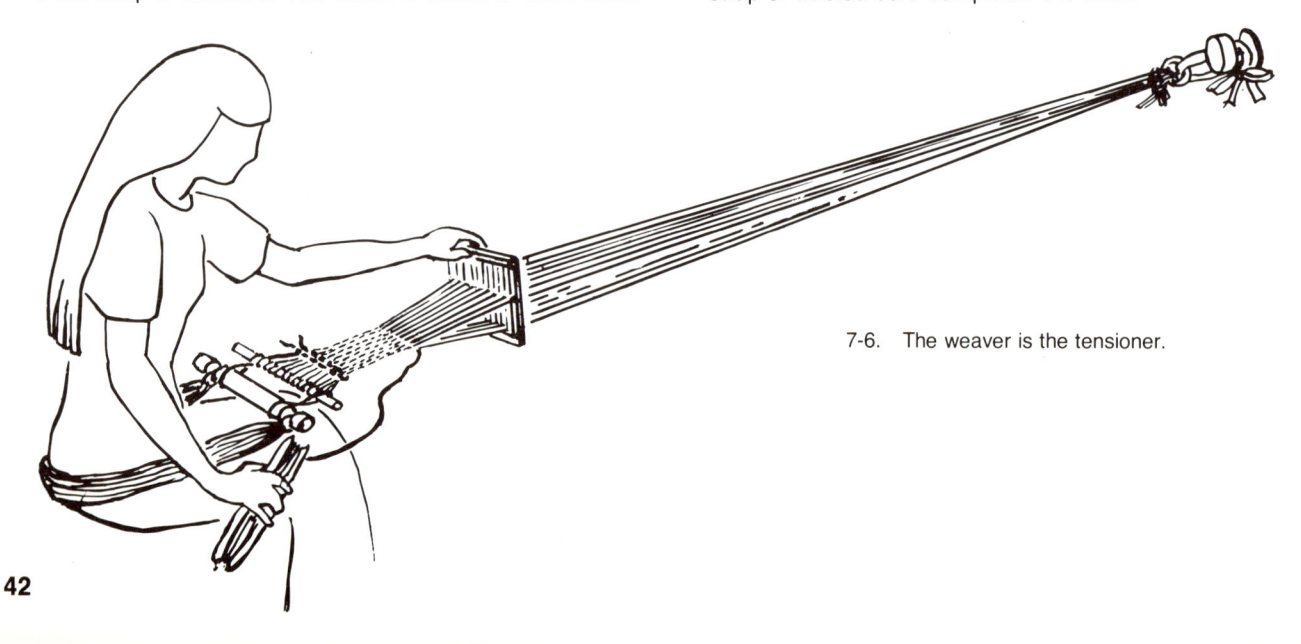

7-6. The weaver is the tensioner.

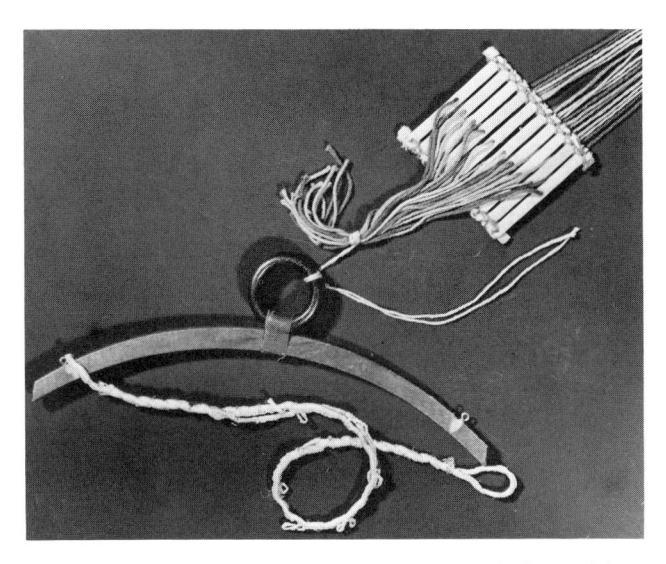

7-8. This backstrap loom was made with easy-to-find materials.

7-10. The linen table runners, designed by Margaret Collins, demonstrate a simple but effective use of woven bands.

The threads of the warp are drawn through the eyes and slots of the rigid heddle — also called the heddle reed — in the chosen pattern order and then secured to the cloth dowel in front of the weaver. The job of threading the loom can be made easy if you use a reed hook. You can make the hook from a wire twist-tie, after you have peeled part of the paper back, or you can use a safety pin with a bent dulled point. Just heat the end of the safety pin so that you can bend it with pliers. (Figure 7–9.) A small crochet hook will also do for a reed hook.

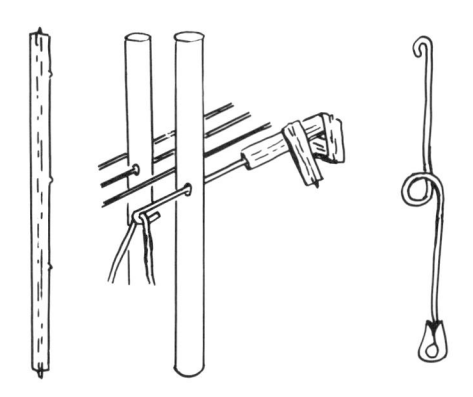

7-9. The reed hook made of wire twist-tie will draw the thread through the heddle eye, as shown in the middle drawing. At right, a safety pin also becomes a reed hook.

In the first project — a two-color pattern that will be simple to thread — you will be able to turn a very ordinary table runner into something original and personal with only a small outlay of yarn. You might want to decorate a tablecloth or place mats instead of the runner; just remember to use yarns that are compatible with the cloth. The runner in Figure 7–10 is made of coarse linen, so perle cotton No. 3 was used. For a close look at the pattern in the center section of the band, see Figure 7–12.

The first step will be to measure the length of the runner. Since you will make two identical bands, allow for double the amount of yarn needed for one band. Our runner will be 50" long, so if you measure the warp threads about two yards long, you will have plenty to allow for shrinkage, take-up, and fringes. After weaving, the bands were washed to preshrink them before they were sewn to the runner.

For those who are unfamiliar with the word "warp" used as a verb, "to warp" means to wind the warp threads, measure them, prepare them for the loom, and thread them on the loom. In this project a warping device will help you to measure each thread accurately. You might turn a card table upside down and wind the thread from leg to leg to measure it. Or else you can make a warping board out of a board about 40" long and 6" wide. If you have a drill, make holes large enough to insert ¾" dowels or pegs, or you can nail them to the board. Place the dowels on the board so that you can

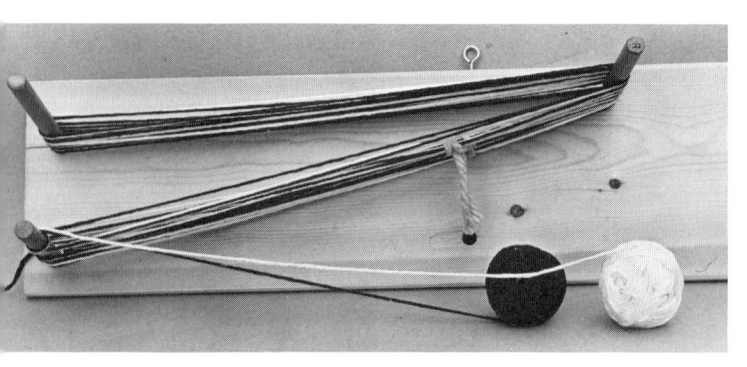

7-11. In the warping board, the ¾" dowels should be set one yard apart, with the two placed at one end 4" to 5" apart.

warp two yards at a time. (Figure 7–11.) Still another warping system would be two chairs set the proper distance from each other. Weight them with bricks or books, so that they won't slip.

There are 51 threads in this pattern, 33 of a light color and 18 a dark color. Each thread is to be two yards long. To wind the threads, take a ball or tube of thread, tie one end to a peg, table, or chair back and then with the ball or tube of yarn in your hand, carry the yarn around the peg at the opposite end of the warping board and back to the peg across from the starter peg, around this peg, back the length of the board to the single peg, and back to the starter peg. You have now wound and measured four yards of yarn or thread, or two warp threads, two yards long each. Continue winding this way until all 33 light threads have been wound. Then remove these from the warping board and wind the 18 dark-colored threads you will need for this pattern. After removing the second set of threads from the warping board, tie one end of all the warps in a strong knot. This will be the end that you tie to the hitching post. Your hitching post can be a door knob, the deck rail of a house or boat, or a tree.

Because there are 51 threads in this pattern, you will need a rigid heddle with at least 26 holes and 25 slots (or 26 slots and 25 holes). To thread this pattern in the rigid heddle, cut the loop of threads at the opposite end from the ones tied to the hitching post and prepare to thread them one by one

7-12. Threading pattern for the table-runner band.

through slot and hole across the rigid heddle. Whether you start in the hole or the slot doesn't make any difference in the finished pattern. Commence threading at one end of the rigid heddle and place the threads in sequence according to the pattern in Figure 7–12. The first dark thread goes in the first opening in your rigid heddle — the slot or the hole, whichever comes first — the second dark thread in the next opening. For example, if you start your first dark thread in a hole, then the second dark thread will be threaded through a slot, the third dark thread in a hole and so on until all the threads have been placed through the rigid heddle in the indicated order. In Figure 7–12 the two lines of squares represent the sequence of the holes and slots across the rigid heddle, with the square at the end of the first line as the mid-warp thread.

As you bring the threads through the holes or slots, tie them to the dowel in groups of 4 to 8 threads, or if you use curtain rings like those in Figure 7–8 you can tie all of the threads in a knot and the knot to the curtain rings. Tie all knots firmly because you will put quite a bit of pull on the weaving and you don't want any of the warp threads to break. Seine twine or wrapping cord are good choices for tying cords.

Strap the backstrap around your lower waist or upper hip and adjust yourself so that you put the warp under tension. Then adjust the rigid heddle so that it is a sufficient distance from the dowel, curtain ring, or whatever cloth stick you have chosen; the object is to form a good shed in between. (See Figure 7–6.)

For band weaving on the rigid heddle no spacers are needed to hold the threads in position, but if you wish to use your rigid heddle for wide weaving in which the full width of the heddle is needed, you can maintain the width and keep the threads evenly spaced when you weave by making your first two weft passages with a heavy yarn or two small dowels or slats of wood.

To weave, push the heddle *down* with one hand, forcing the threads in the holes to a lower position than those in the slots. Insert one weft shot with each shed change. The threads in the holes are the moving threads while those in the slots remain stationary. (Figure 7–13.) You then change the shed by lifting the heddle *up* so that the threads in the holes are higher than those in the slots. Push the threads as close together as possible so that as you weave the shape of the band is being formed above the space you leave for fringe.

Wind sufficient weft on your shuttle so that you won't have to splice as you weave. To figure out what will be adequate,

44

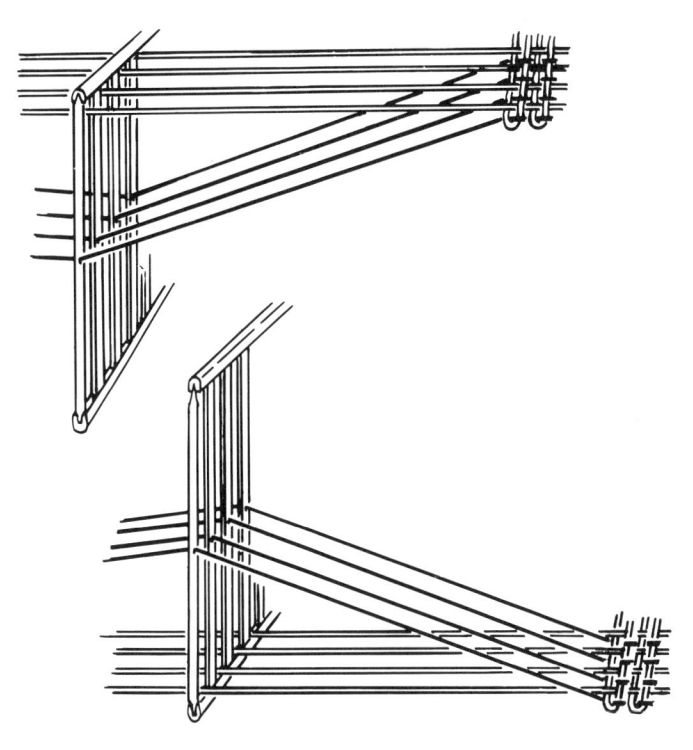

7-13. Changing the shed, or making the shed, is accomplished by pushing the heddle down, at left, or pulling it up, at right.

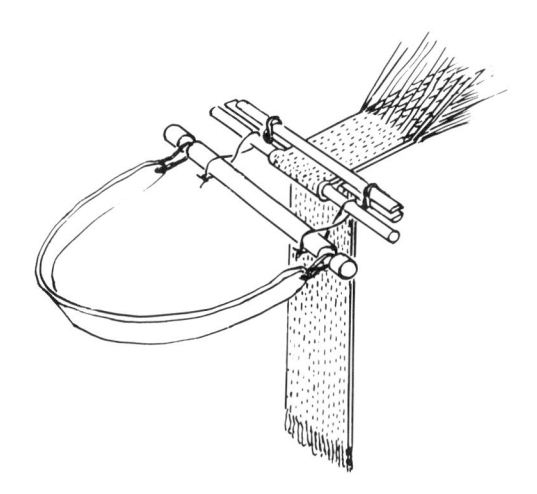

7-14. Holding the finished weaving firmly.

7-15. The finished weaving goes down through both curtain rings, then over one, under the other, and over the top of the upper ring to hold it firm while the weaving continues.

you must first decide on the width of the band. In this project, the band is about two and a half inches wide. Multiply the width by the finished length of the band; then multiply that figure by the number of weft shots per inch. The number of shots per inch do vary, but try to keep them the same. We made about six shots to the inch on this cotton band. It won't be long before you are able to calculate weft more precisely according to the width of the band, the thickness of the weft, the size of the warp threads, and the closeness of beat.

Make the first weft shot, leaving a tail of weft sticking out, to weave in with the next few shots. Remember to keep your selvedges firm and the width of your band uniform.

When the weaving has progressed to a point where it is too long to reach and still make a good shed, loosen the backstrap, untie the front end of the warp threads, and lay the finished weaving over the dowel, holding it firmly. Place two flat sticks or rulers over the weaving and lash them together with rubber bands or string to hold the woven band firmly between them. (Figure 7–14.) Figure 7–15 shows how the curtain rings perform the same function as the dowel and stick arrangement. When the band is long enough, some weavers just wrap it around their waists and use it for the backstrap. Refasten the backstrap and continue weaving.

When the band is long enough for the table runner, cut the weft, leaving a tail of about five inches. In addition to weaving the weft back into the band you can also machine stitch the ends for a band edge that will not ravel.

The rigid heddle stretcher frame shown in Figure 7–16 takes the back out of backstrap weaving. It puts the warp into one complete unit, one that can be left for a moment or a week without disturbing the tension or the weaving. We designed it for our own use and then discovered it made an ideal demonstration loom for schoolchildren to watch and to

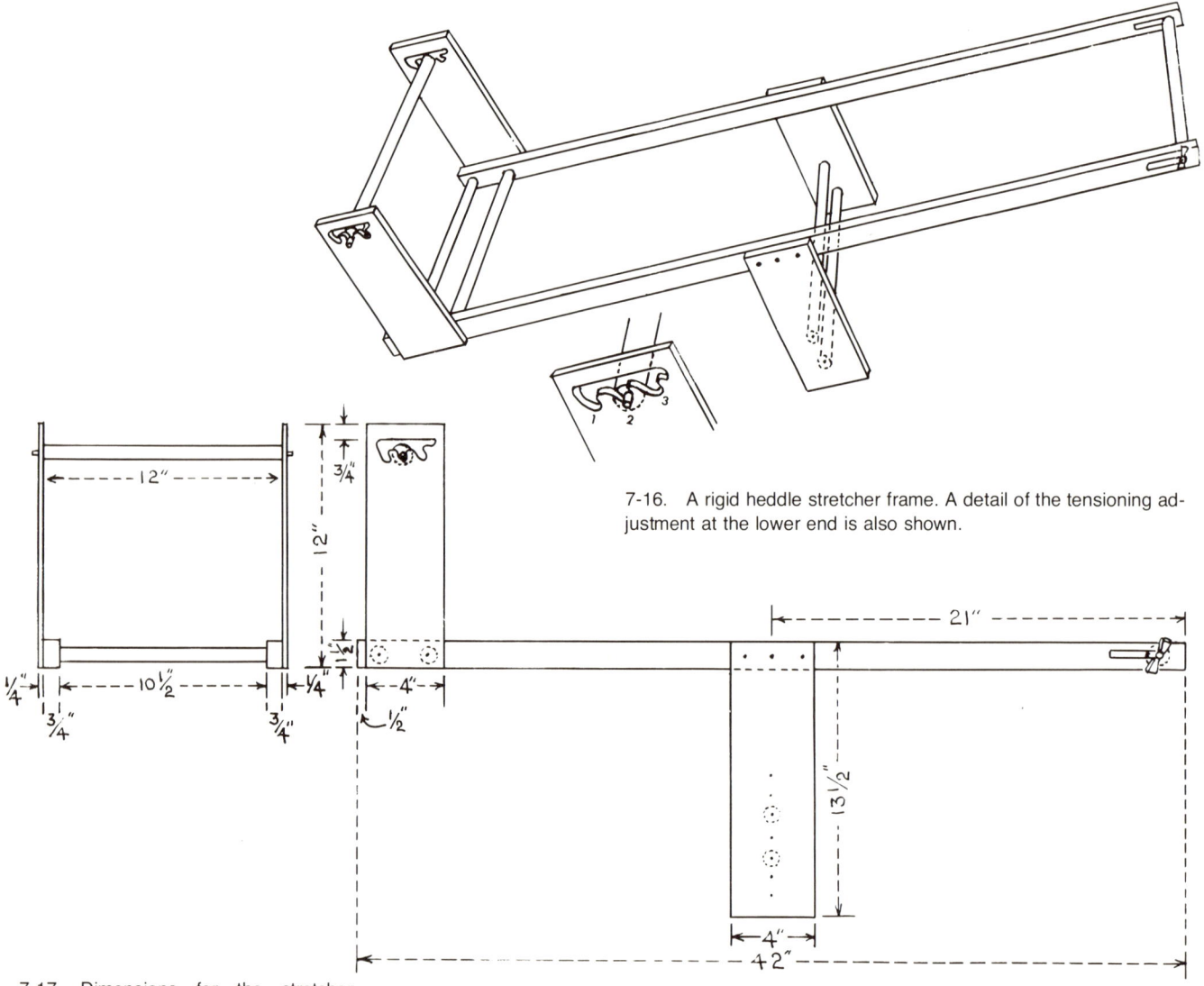

7-16. A rigid heddle stretcher frame. A detail of the tensioning adjustment at the lower end is also shown.

7-17. Dimensions for the stretcher frame.

weave on. Capable of being adapted to card weaving as well as tapestry and narrow woven fabrics, it can accommodate two tensioning adjustments. One is at the top, where a dowel is held with a wing nut in an open groove, and the other is at the lower end.

Figure 7-17 shows the general structure of the loom with suggested dimensions. To build the frame, you will need 2 1" x 2" standard cut boards, 2 pieces of ¼" plywood, 4" wide and 12" long for the lower front section, and 2 pieces of 4" x 13½" plywood for the feet. You will also need three ¾" dowels, 11" long; three ¾" dowels, 12" long; eight 1½" wood screws; eight ¾" wood screws; two ¼" lag screws; and two ¼" wing nuts. The ends of the dowels should be predrilled to facilitate installing the screws. One set of plywood boards makes the uprights for the front of the loom and the other set makes the feet of the loom — to be installed at the center of the 1" x 2" boards on the outside, joined together with the 12" dowels, and held in place with the screws. The extra holes in a row on the plywood feet are for bracing the dowels or for installing extra dowels.

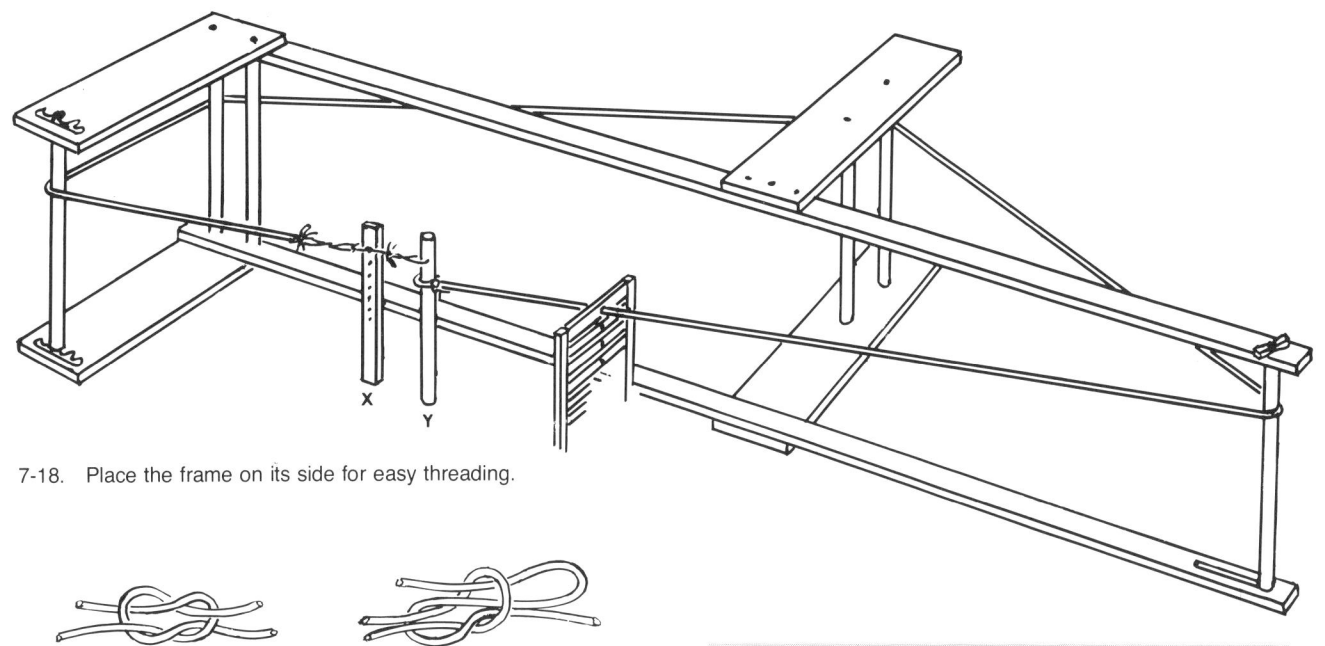

7-18. Place the frame on its side for easy threading.

7-19. At left, a granny knot; at right, a square knot with one end looped, so that it will untie easily.

Although the frame takes up only a small amount of space, it can hold up to 80 inches of warp. You can wind the warp on a warping board, premeasuring and precutting it just as you did with the backstrap loom system. Look at Figure 7–18 to see how the frame is set up for warping. Fasten the tie-bar X (see Figure 7–1) to the cloth dowel Y with a cord threaded through holes drilled in the dowel and the tie-bar, so that the warp can be tied to the dowel and then threaded through the heddle, go around the frame, and be tied to the tie-bar, ready for weaving. Use a knot like the two shown in Figure 7–19, or any knot that holds firmly and unties easily, to secure the warp. To keep the rigid heddle from swinging around while you thread, tie on the first and last threads of the band at each side of the heddle first. The tie-bar is a strip of wood about 1″ wide and as long as the cloth dowel or as wide as the rigid heddle. It has holes drilled about ¼″ apart through which you tie strong cords, leaving 3″ ends for tying the warps.

In a first project with this frame, you can use cotton rug yarn or wool or acrylic knitting yarns; we used four-ply knitting worsted to make a yardstick sheath similar to those shown in Figure 7–20. The finished length of the band, before it is

7-20. Bands were shaped into a variety of yardstick sheaths.

47

folded, is 70–76 inches; the sides will be whipped together. To hang the sheath easily you can sew a ring on the back or attach the ring to the top.

We will use a two-color pattern with 28 dark threads, 17 light threads — 2½ yards long to allow for take-up in the weaving and fringe — and a weft of slightly contrasting color so that it can be easily seen at the edges when you sew the sheath together. The rigid heddle for this pattern needs at least 23 holes and 22 slots to accommodate the 45 yarns. (If your rigid heddle has more slots and holes than you need, balance the pattern in the center holes and slots, leaving an equal number of empty ones on each side.) The threading draft for this pattern is shown below.

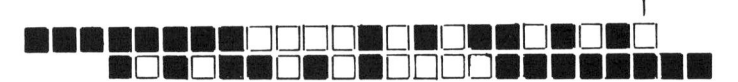

7-21. The pattern for the yardstick sheath in Figure 7–22.

Tie the premeasured and precut yarns to the dowel Y as shown in Figure 7–18. Keeping them in the sequence of the pattern, thread them one by one through hole and slot before you bring them around the loom frame. After the thread has gone through the heddle, from front to back, tie it to one of the threads attached to the tie-bar with a knot similar to the one illustrated in Figure 7–19. The knot you use should be easy to untie, in case you have to adjust tension on an individual thread, but it will hold firm when tied; you might, for example, use a bow knot with a single loop.

For cotton yarns, put the tensioning dowel in slot number 1 (see Figure 7–16); this affords the greatest tension and the thread can be loosened as the weaving progresses and the yarns begin to take up. With wools, put the tensioning dowel in the middle slot so tension can be tightened or loosened according to the way the yarn behaves. The dowel held with the wing nut at the top of the frame can be adjusted for very fine control of tensioning.

After all the threads have been warped through the heddle and tied to the tie-bar, you are ready to weave. The dowel should be in front of the rigid heddle toward you, just like the dowel or curtain ring in backstrap weaving. The tie-bar is behind the rigid heddle and below the dowel.

Push the threads on the front dowel close together. (Figure 7–22.) You weave the same way you would if you were using the backstrap system except that when the weaving is too far away from you to make a good shed, you release one of the tensioning dowels, pull the weaving down toward you, tighten the tension, and continue weaving.

7-22. Anchor the threads to the cloth stick and push them close together to make the most use of your warp.

To finish the band, you can weave a few inches of weft back up, row by row, with a needle or use the following method, which will give you a fourth selvedge on the end of your band. This method is suitable for any woven band that uses yarn for weft. When you use other materials for weft — bamboo, grasses, or unspun wool, for example — you could knot the fringe ends or brush a little fabric glue along the bottom of the weaving.

To make a fourth selvedge, cut three or more pieces of thin, strong thread, five or six times the width of the band when looped in half. (Figure 7–23.) At the point where the weaving is approximately within an inch of completion, take the first looped thread and lay it in the shed along with the

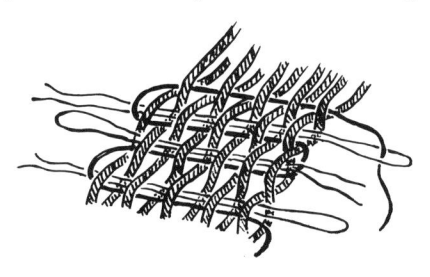

7-23

48

weft thread. When the shuttle is moving the weft from left to right, the looped end of the cord will be on the left side.

Now change the shed and place the next looped cord in this shed along with the weft, leaving the looped end sticking out of the opposite side. Continue laying in the cords on opposite sides until the weaving is finished. After the last loop is in place, make one more shot, ending at the same edge of the band as the last looped cord. Leave a weft end five to six times the width of the band.

Now you are ready to weave the weft-end back up into the band. Tuck the end through the loop on the last cord, grasp the two loose ends of the cord, and gently draw cord and weft through the woven fabric and out the other side. Repeat this procedure from side to side until all the looped cords have served their purpose of weaving the weft back into the band. After you have clipped off the remaining bit of weft, the band is ready to be used with no further knotting or stitching. Cut the band from the tie-bar and the dowel and pull the short fringes through the heddle. Lace the two sides together, weft to weft, making one side a few inches longer than the other so that the top of the yardstick will show.

Instead of sewing the ring or buckle on your band, you can weave it on by planning the warp sequence so that each thread is doubled over the ring or buckle, through the center,

7-24. A small cotton belt with a plain stripe pattern is being woven over two small rings.

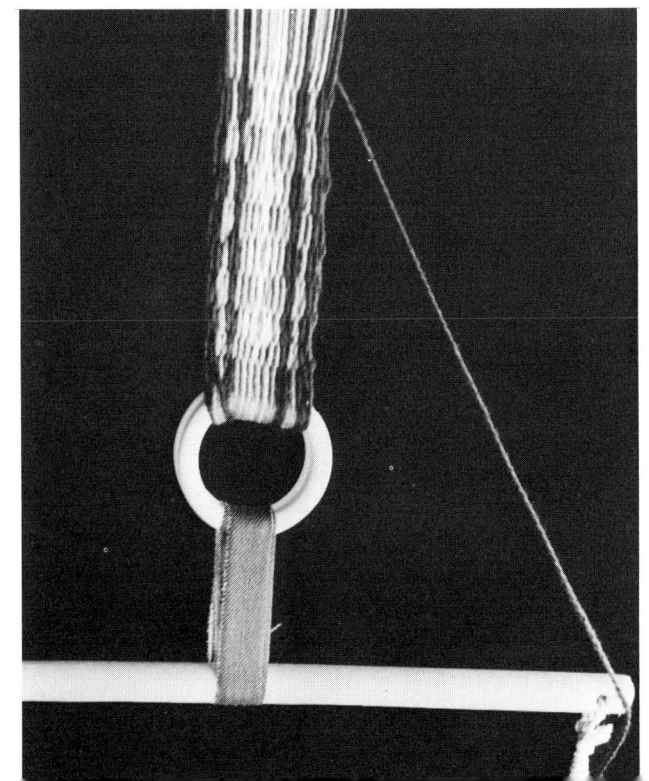

leaving the tongue free. In the small cotton belt in Figure 7–24 we used two little rings for the buckle.

To make this belt, first tape the buckle, double rings, or single ring to the front dowel with cloth or strong masking tape. (Figure 7–25.) Measure and cut the yarns 2 yards long for a finished belt of 24" to 26". Cut each yarn twice the length needed so it can be doubled over the rings. Also, doubling the yarn and using two ends as one — placing two ends in each hole and slot — will make the pattern easy to follow and to thread.

7-25. The buckle or ring will stay in place during the threading if you thread the two outside pairs of warps first.

For this pattern, which uses 14 dark-plum color, 14 medium blue, and 5 light-yellow yarns, your rigid heddle should have 33 slots and holes. Remember to double each yarn over the rings and count each doubled thread as *one* in

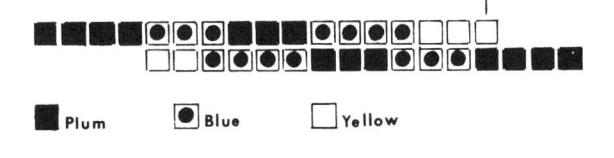

■ Plum   ◉ Blue   ☐ Yellow

7-26. Pattern draft for the belt in Figure 7–24.

the pattern. The threading draft for this pattern is shown in Figure 7–26.

Note in Figure 7–25 that the two outside plum-colored pairs of thread are threaded first, to keep the rigid heddle steady for the rest of the threading if you are using a frame like the one in Figure 7–16. If you are threading backstrap-style, however, follow the threading instructions in the first project — the bands for the table runner.

Always loop the yarns the same way from the same side of the buckle or ring so that they will not be twisted. Weave as before, pushing the rigid heddle down for one shed and weft shot, and up for the next. Weave until your belt is the desired length. Measure it with the tension released because the finished belt off tension may be shorter than while on tension; some yarns stretch under tension.

Finish the end of the belt in the same way you did the yardstick sheath. Another way of finishing is to clip the two outside warps with every other weft shot and weave them in, thus bringing the belt to a point. Stitch the end on the sewing machine or dip it in fabric glue to keep it from raveling. (Figure 7–27.)

7-27. A way to finish the band.

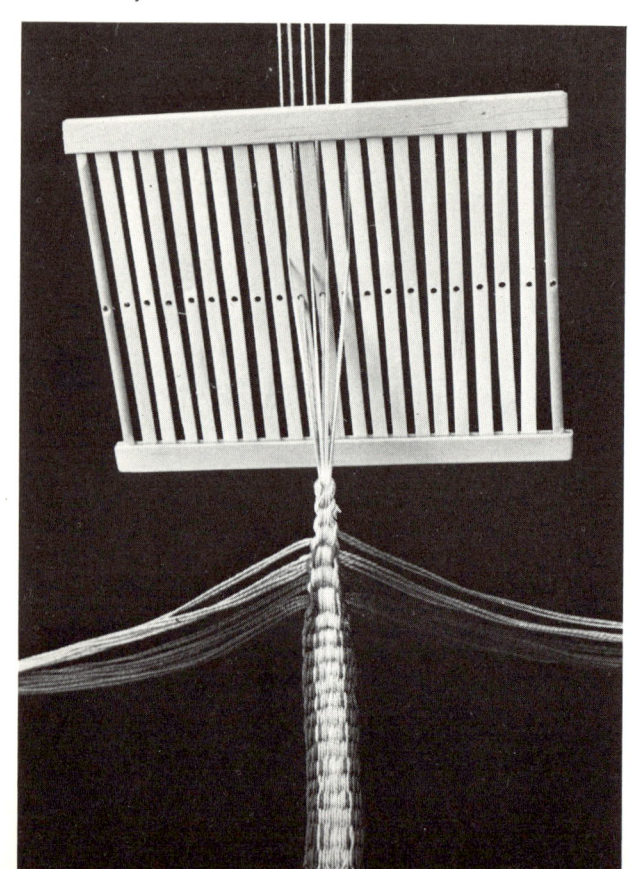

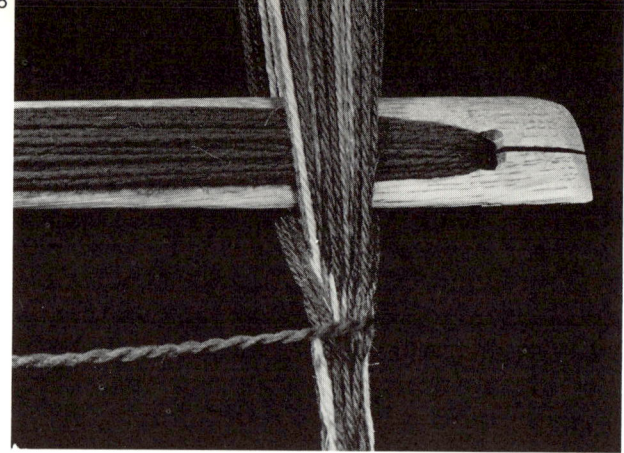

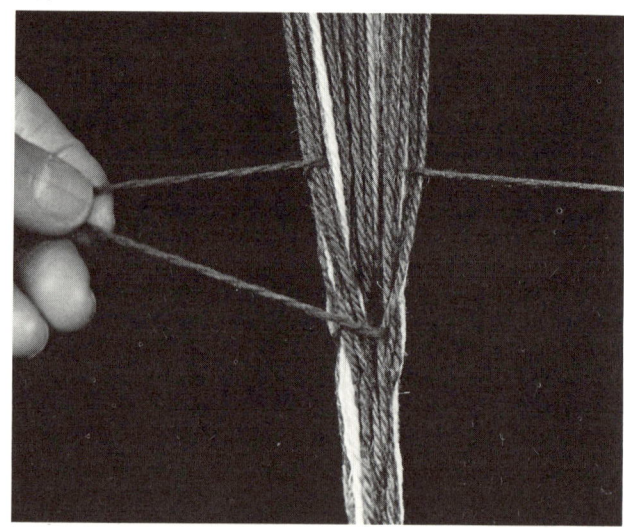

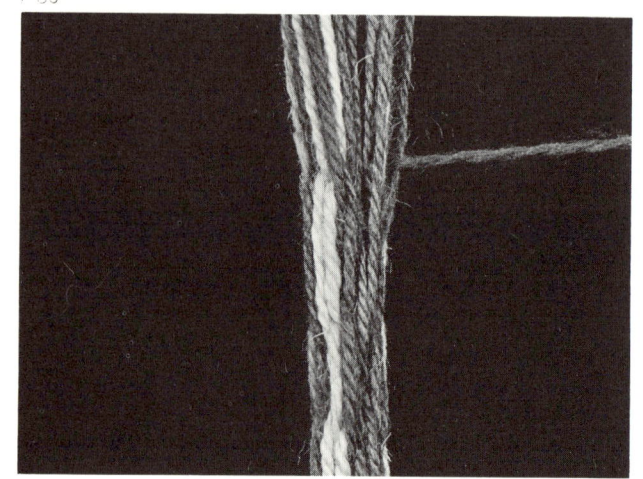

7-28, 7-29, and 7-30. Making a strong tubular band. Figure 7–30 gives a closer view of the band taking shape.

The bag in Figure C-8 of the color section was made of two rigid heddle bands, with the top band tapering into a tubular weaving for use as a shoulder strap. You can convert a flat band to a tube or cylinder by inserting the weft from one side of the band only. (Figures 7–28, 7–29, and 7–30.) Pull the weft quite snugly with each shed change and the round tube will take shape.

For experienced band weavers who want to make a bag like this one, you would have to sew the bands to each other in a spiral. Start with the bottom of the bag, by folding the first end of the first band in half. Fold it at an angle and begin joining at the fringed end. This gives a solid bottom instead of a seam, which might weaken with use. (Figure 7–31.) As you sew the spiral, you determine the bag's shape. It can be long and narrow, or wide and short, or wide at the bottom and narrow on top or vice versa. At the top of the bag, loop the handle over and stitch it to the opposite side to make a shoulder strap. Figure 7–32 shows one way to finish the end of the strap: Wrap the fringes of the handle part way, skip part of the fringe, leaving it unwrapped, then wrap another portion. In this fashion, you have made a buttonhole to use in fastening the handle. (See pages 76–78 and Figure 10–3 for wrapping instructions.)

To extend design and color capabilities, you might experiment with using two rigid heddles threaded together on one loom. We have simplified the instructions so that your initiation into this form of weaving won't be discouraging. Once you are familiar with the principles involved, your imagination will direct you along other paths of investigation and creativity.

For the first project, which is designed to give you some experience with the procedure, use short lengths of yarn, about one and one-half yards long. The two rigid heddles will be called the *back* reed and the *front* reed. (Figure 7–33.) Use at least two different colors and two different weights of yarn.

Start with the back reed, and thread each hole and slot with a heavy yarn; knitting worsted will be fine. Then in each slot of the back reed place two finer threads of contrasting colors; a fingering yarn will give you a contrasting weight. In our sample we used a heavy gold yarn and a fine gold and orange yarn.

If you are working alone, wedge the back reed between two heavy books on a flat surface to hold it motionless while you thread the front reed. Start at one side of the back reed and take the first heavy wool from the first hole and one fine

7-31. Starting a spiral bagged end.

7-32. Finishing the bag strap.

thread from the first slot and pass these two threads through the first slot in the front reed. Next, take the heavy thread from the first slot in the back reed and place it by itself through the next hole in the front reed. Notice that for the back reed you commence threading in the *hole,* whereas for the front reed you ignore the first hole and commence threading in the first slot. You are now ready for the next slot in the front reed.

There is one thread left in the first slot of the back reed. Take this thread, plus the next heavy yarn (in the second hole), plus one fine thread from the second slot in the rear heddle reed and place all three threads together in the next

7-33. Threading two rigid heddles. The reed on the left is the *back* reed and the one on the right is the *front* reed.

slot in the front reed. The formula is: one heavy thread in each hole; one heavy and two fine in each slot. The fine threads split or separate when they move from the back reed to the front reed, and the heavy threads move from the hole in the back reed to the slot in the front reed and from the slot in the back reed to the hole in the front reed. It will soon be apparent that we suggested you use heavy and fine threads as a means of clarifying the instructions. After a few practice sessions, you will begin to see the possibilities for experimentation.

To weave with two rigid heddles, follow these steps: Lift the back heddle and make one weft shot, using the fine yarn for weft. Push both heddles down and insert the weft shot. Lift the front heddle and make a weft shot. Push both heddles down and make the weft shot. Repeat these steps until you finish the band. Weaving with two rigid heddles produces a two-faced band, such as the one in C-9 in the color section.

We have mentioned preshrinking bands before applying them to other fabrics, but some synthetic fibers will actually stretch in the weaving process, so make allowances for these yarn characteristics when you measure the threads for your bands.

Broken warp threads need not be a problem in weaving. When a thread breaks in the warp, you can mend it by first tracing it back to the dowel to which it was tied. Measure off a matching thread a few inches longer than the broken thread.

7-34. The division of the warps which produces the double faces of the band is shown.

7-35. Mending a broken warp: a. Fasten the end with a pin. b. Weave the new warp down into the weaving a few rows.

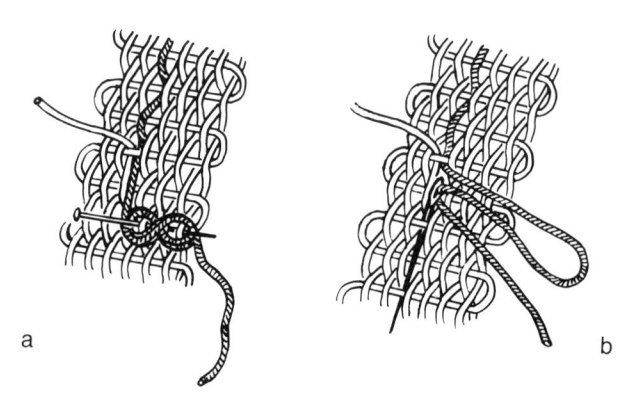

a

b

Tie the new thread securely in place of the broken one, remove the broken one, and retrace the path of the broken warp back down through the rigid heddle to the point of the break. Fasten the loose end of the new warp by winding it figure-eight fashion around a pin inserted a few inches below the weaving edge, down into the band. If you don't want to risk a hole in your hand, remove the pin after you have woven a few shots to catch the new thread. Thread a needle with the loose warp end you have removed from the pin and weave it down a few shots farther into the woven band to anchor and conceal it. (Figure 7–35.) You may want to wait until the band is finished to do the mending, but sometimes it is easier to make this finishing while the warp is under tension. You can mend any broken warp on any loom in this way; just suit the tying on of the new warp to the loom you are using.

Figure 7–36 shows a variety of designs you can achieve if you follow the corresponding pattern drafts in Figure 7–37. These pattern drafts can be used for inkle-loom weaving as well as for the rigid heddle. The first square represents your first thread and the second square your second thread. Keep on threading straight across the loom, from hole to slot, on the rigid heddle. On the inkle loom, thread the "open" or shed thread and then the heddle thread. The dotted line marks the mid-warp thread and is there to help you check the pattern.

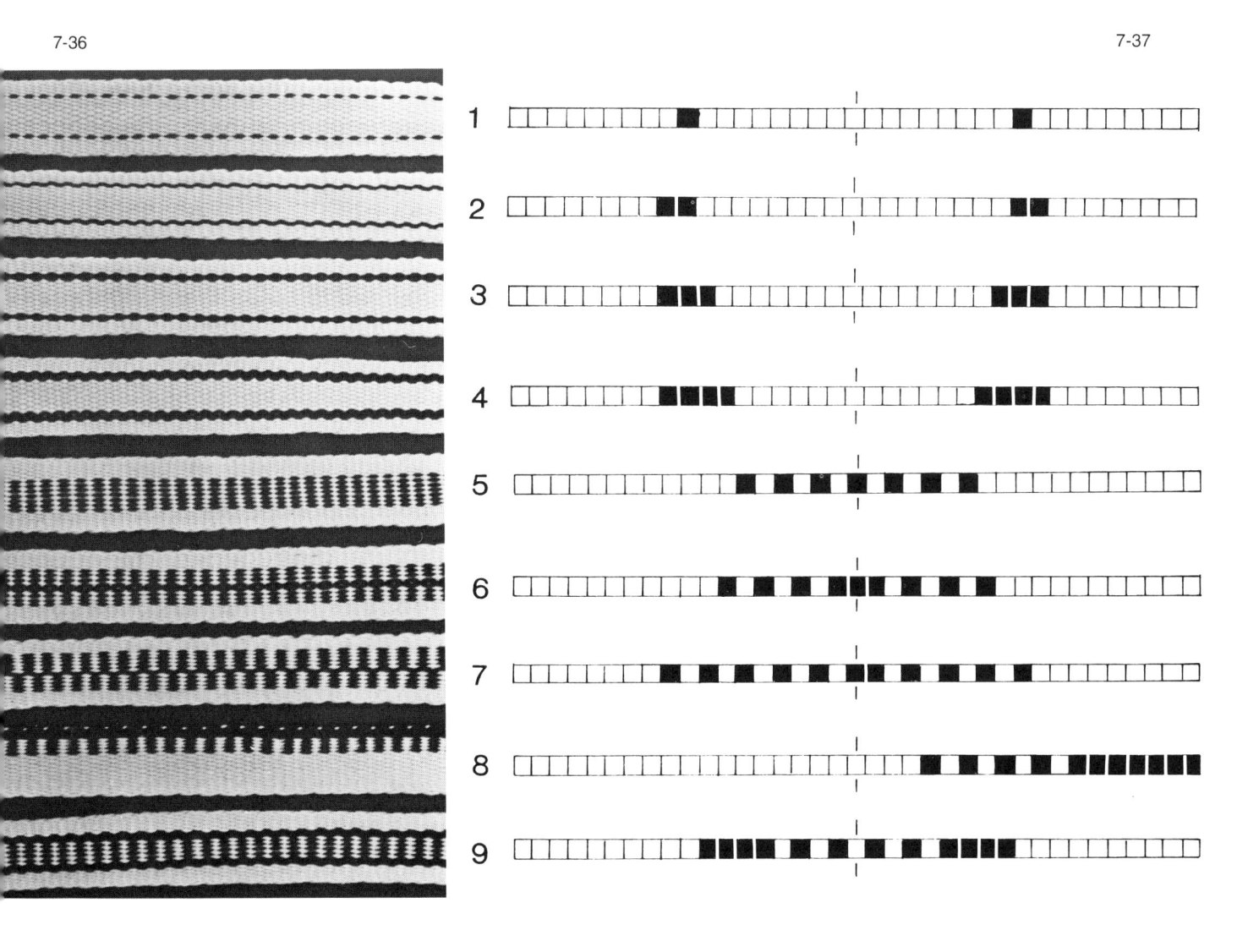

7-36

7-37

8.
band weaving on the american inkle loom

About thirty years ago, E. E. Gilmore of Stockton, California, designed and began to manufacture the weaving structure we call the "inkle" loom. Derived from the English inkle loom, Gilmore's model was much more portable than the bulkier floor frame from which it was adapted. Since then the design has been altered from time to time depending upon the builder, but the essential structure remains the same. The basic components of the loom consist of a base approximately twenty to thirty inches long and a durable upright section to hold the major pegs. The pegs are generally made of ¾" to one-inch doweling, but could be metal rods if you wished. If you want to build an inkle loom, you can follow the measurements in Figure 8–1. The loom shown was made of 1" plywood in one piece and the ¾" or 1" dowels were cut 6" long.

An essential part of the loom is the tensioner, which should

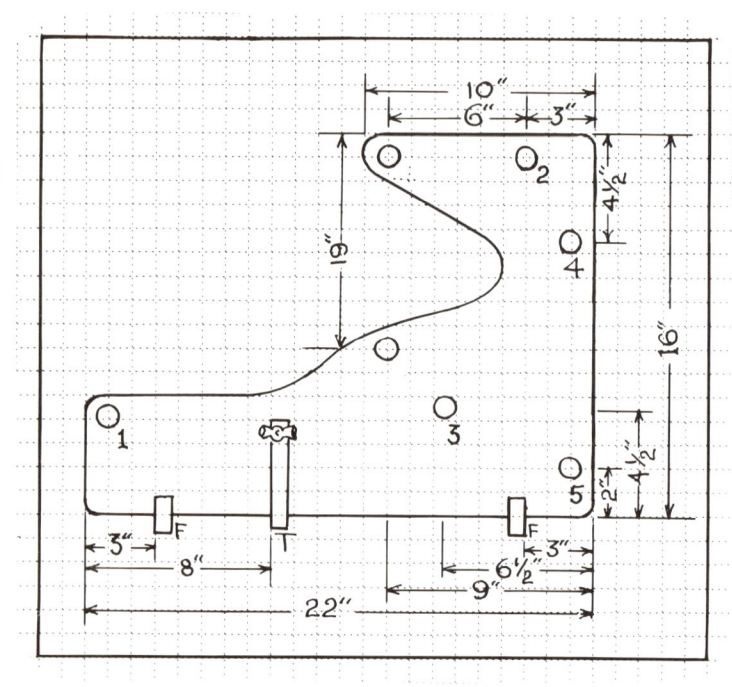

8-1. This model of the American inkle loom was designed by Virginia Joy.

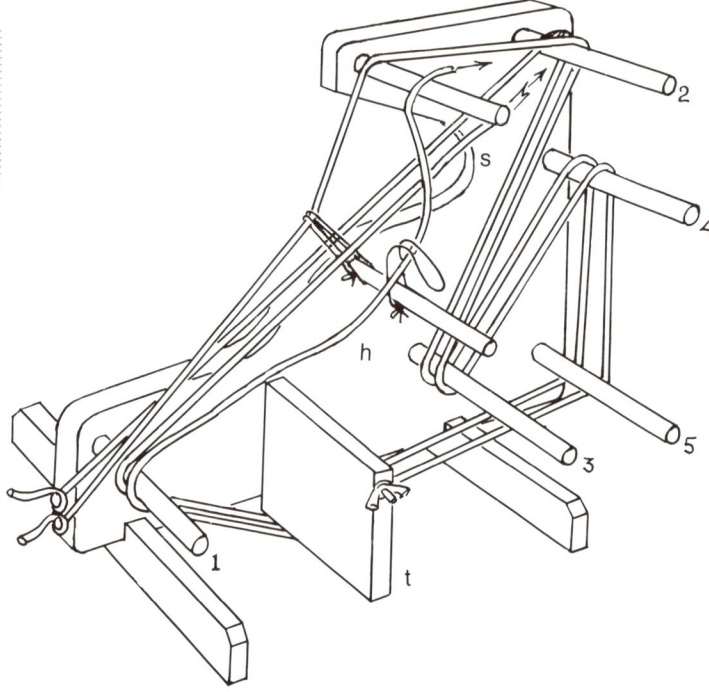

8-2. Threading diagram for the Virginia Joy inkle loom.

be fastened to the loom in such a way as to be easily loosened or tightened as needed. The tension board in Figure 8–2 is fastened with an eight-inch machine bolt and secured with a lock washer and a wing nut. Other means of tensioning may be devised, such as movable pegs, but the adjustment is not quite as fine as that achieved by a friction tensioner.

In the inkle loom, half of the warp threads are passed through or held by means of a string heddle, so that the two sheds are easily separated for weaving. There are several ways of making heddles, but the simplest and speediest way is to use the two center pegs of the loom, one above the other, as a gauge for tying the heddle.

We have listed several supply sources in the back of the book where looms can be bought. If you make your own inkle loom, build it with a good tensioning device and strong parts, so it will hold together under strain. As mentioned before, you can use any of the patterns for rigid heddle bands on the inkle loom. On both these looms you can also use the pick-up patterns described later in this chapter.

For your first band on an inkle loom select one of the two-color patterns for rigid heddle weaving given at the end of chapter 7 so that you can practice threading your inkle loom. (See Figure 7–37.) Start by making the heddles as shown in Figure 8–3. Tie each string — using either crochet cotton, seine twine, wrapping twine, carpet warp, or any non-fuzzy cotton yarn or string — around the two pegs one above the other to ensure that all the heddles will be the same size. Note the rubber bands on the peg ends which act as stoppers and prevent the warp threads from slipping off. Make at least 20 string heddles.

The tensioner T should be set in the proper position for the yarn you will be using. Some threads will tend to stretch — some wools and acrylics for example — during the weaving process and others will take up or tighten (cotton or linen). If you are using a yarn that tends to stretch, set the tensioner tilted back at about a 45° angle. For a yarn that doesn't stretch, keep the tensioner vertical; in this way the tension can be released later from time to time, since the weaving process will increase the overall warp tension.

A characteristic of the inkle looms is the continuous warp, so be sure that none of the yarns are tied to the pegs during weaving. You have two pathways to follow in threading the loom: One group of threads will be called the "heddle" threads and the other group will be called the "open" or shed

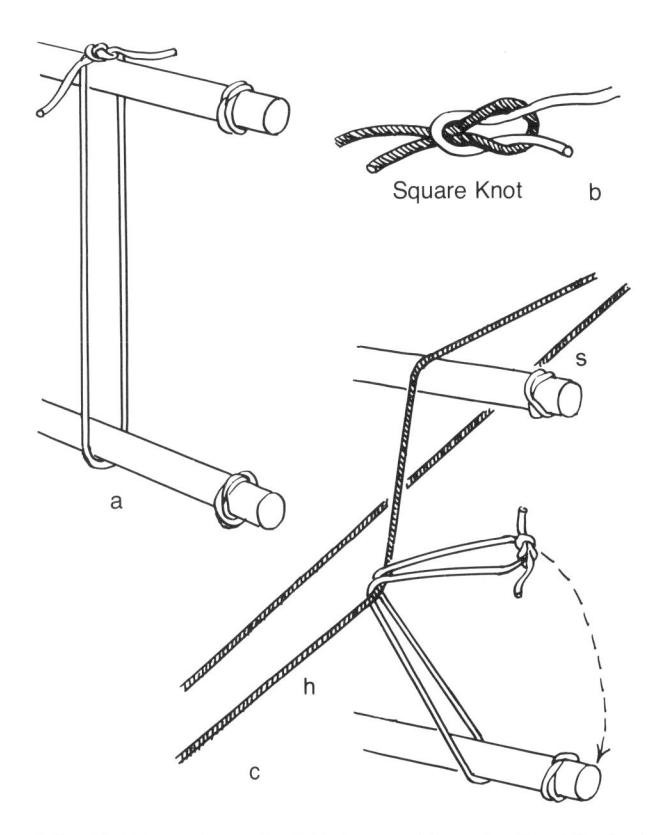

8-3. Heddle-making on the inkle loom: a. Measuring the string heddles. b. A square knot that can be used to tie the heddle. c. Securing the heddle thread with the heddle.

threads. This is the basic division of threads that will apply to any inkle loom.

Follow the threading diagram in Figure 8–2. If you wanted to maintain a solid color along the outside edge of the band, you would make the first three "rounds" (the term for one complete path of the warp yarn around the loom) with your first color and the fourth round with your second color. As you start each new thread, fasten the beginning end of the yarn to the front of the loom temporarily with tape or a thumbtack and leave a short tail to be tied later.

The *open* thread goes under the top center peg and the *heddle* thread goes over the top peg and is caught and held with one of the string heddles. Always begin and end each band with an open thread; it helps to make a smoother selvedge.

Continue threading, following the pattern you have chosen,

8-4. Priscilla Chong weaves on her compact inkle loom.

until all the threads have been warped to the loom. Remove the tape or thumbtack from the thread and the loom, and tie the beginning and end of each color of yarn together to make a continuous warp. Do not tie yarns to any of the pegs, because then the warp will not move around the loom as the weaving progresses. After a few practice bands, you may want to try some patterns using several colors. As you change colors, tie the new color to the end of the previous one and continue to warp the loom. These ends will be cut apart when you are finished and become fringe.

Select a weft of a matching color if you want an invisible edge or a contrasting weft color for a decorative addition to the design. The use of alternating thick and thin weft yarns will add a novel effect to the band. Wind plenty of weft onto a belt shuttle or similar yarn carrier. The general band-weaving instructions given in the previous chapter apply to inkle bands as well as rigid heddle band and they will also pertain to the card-woven bands discussed in the next chapter.

When you weave, you make both sheds with your hands. The open threads move up or down to make the sheds, while the heddle threads remain more or less stationary. Sometimes, with a sticky warp, you have to move the heddle threads back and forth to loosen the warp, but in general the threads remain in place. The first shed is made by inserting the hand between the upper and lower parts of the warp *behind* the heddles and pushing down on the open threads. For the second shed you lift the open threads up. A weft thread is passed through each shed change. (Figures 8–5, 8–6, and 8–7.)

8-5. Push *down* on the open or shed warps to make the first shed.

8-6. *Lift* the open warps to make the second shed.

8-7. *Below:* this is the second shed, with the shed warps up and the weft shuttle passing through the shed.

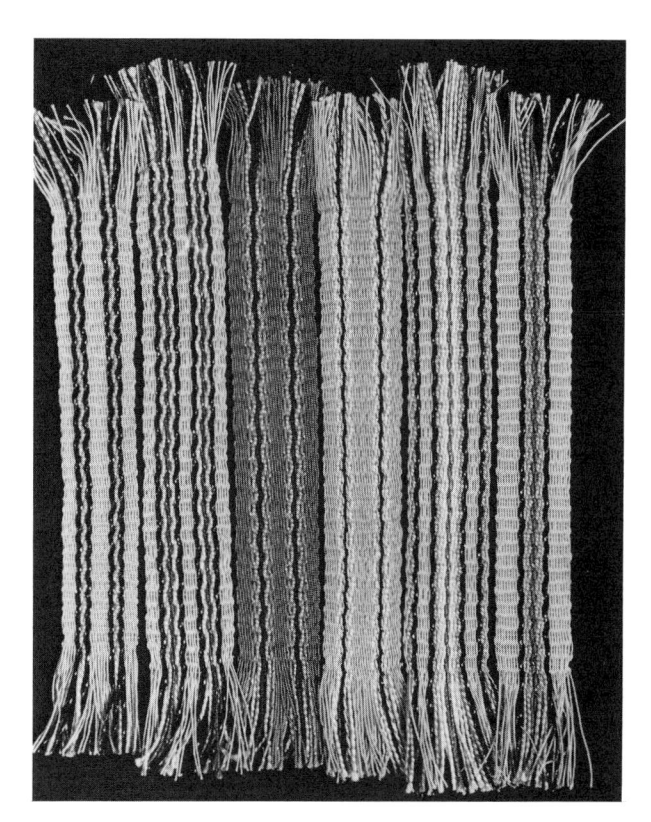

8-8. These small inkle bands made of fine threads and metallic threads were woven in plain weave and used as bookmarks. (Inger Osland, weaver.)

Draw the warp threads close together with the weft yarn and beat down firmly with the shuttle or the side of your hand. When the weaving comes close to the heddles, release the tension and pull the warp toward you as much as is required to make a good shed once more. Keep tension on inkle bands tight so that the threads are close together with no weft showing and beat firmly to keep the pattern close.

Some of the most interesting weaves for inkle bands and rigid heddle bands are the pick-up patterns. You see many of these patterns on belts from Mexico, Tibet, South America, and the north European and Scandinavian countries as well as on cloth from nearly every part of the world. Pick-up is a descriptive term for the process of bringing threads from the lower half of the open shed to the upper half in order to form a design on the top surface of the band. In describing this weaving procedure, the two surfaces of the band, or the two sheds, are referred to as the background or ground shed and the pattern shed, and the warps planned for the pattern which forms a design on the top surface of the band are called pattern warps, while those upon which the design is formed are called background or ground warps and are planned with their role in mind.

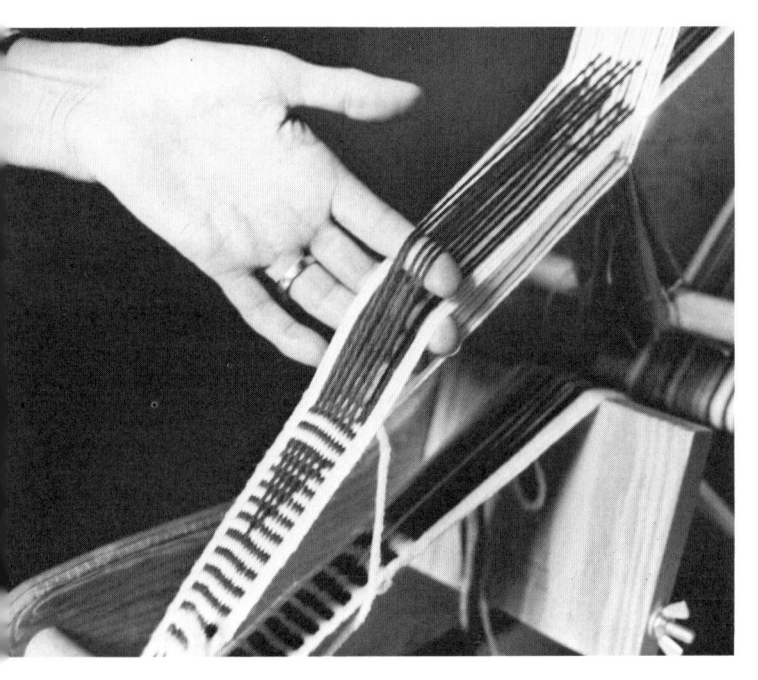

8-9

You can use a small stick, double-pointed knitting needle, or your fingers to make the pick-up. You can reach down from the background shed to the pattern warps below and bring the warps to the surface or you can simply hold them up from the pattern shed, change shed to the background shed, make the weft shot, remove the pick-up stick or your fingers, then change to the pattern warp shed and continue. In Figure 8–9 the pattern shed is up and the fingers are picking up or holding up the threads which will form the design when the background shed is brought to the top.

In general, if you are just beginning to learn pick-up, you will find that the patterns will be easier to see and follow if you use a lightweight yarn of one color for the background warp, and a heavier yarn or double the background weight for the pattern warp. The heavier yarn will show up and cover the background better. Geometric designs such as squares,

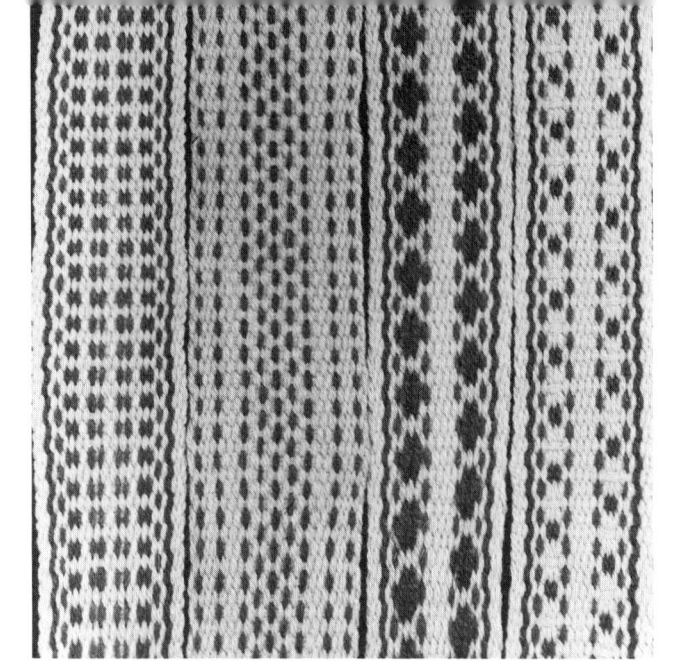

8-10. The two bands on the right show two sides of a simple pick-up pattern made on a patterned warp rather than the plain surface generally used for pick-up.

diamonds, crosses, or X's make good beginning designs for pick-up. The outside edges are usually threaded to a solid stripe or stripes, leaving the center of the band for the pattern. A simple stripe pattern can also be used for easy pick-up. (Figure 8–10.) Patterns may be worked freely on the loom or planned on graph paper first.

You don't want the warp floats to be too long, so the pick-up of an individual thread occurs only once; it will automatically float for three weft shots and then will be held down by the next weft shot. The first time you weave a pick-up pattern you will see what is meant by "automatically floating": the thread is automatically *up* for the two pattern shots before and after the background shot and is held up or picked up when the background shed is made and woven. For example, if the dark threads are your pattern, as in Figure 8–10, then make one weft shot with the dark threads up, keep up (or pick up) the dark pattern threads you will need for your design, change shed to the light, or background threads, weave a shot of weft through the shed — under the light threads and the pattern threads you picked up — change the shed to the dark or pattern threads, and weave. You have actually kept the pattern threads up on the surface of the fabric for three weft shots, making a float over three wefts.

To make the bands for the bag in Figure 8–11, look at the photograph of pattern No. 7 in Figure 8–20 and then at the corresponding diagram in Figure 8–21. Note that in the pat-

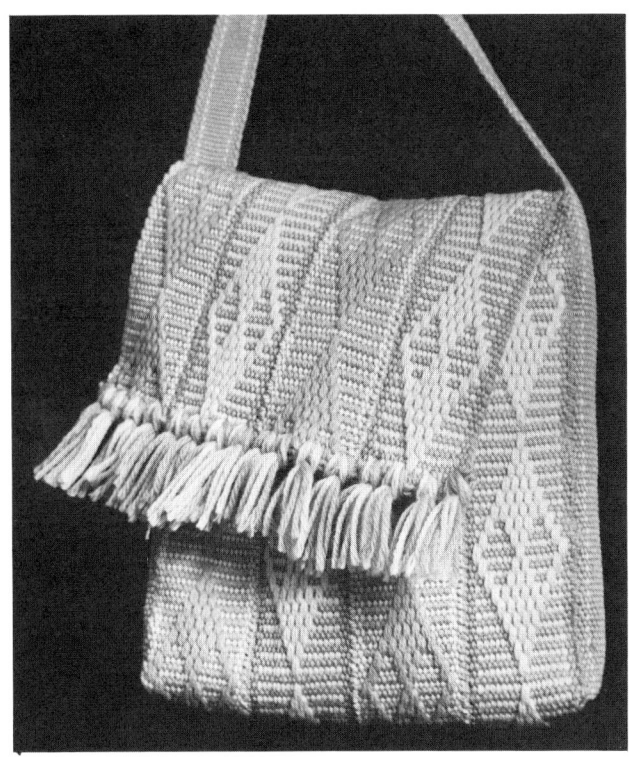

8-11. The shoulder bag achieves a unity of design through its simple geometric pick-up patterns along with the subtle colors of blue on blue. (Woven by Virginia Joy.)

8-12. The inkle-woven band with pick-up pattern is a decorative trim for a wool poncho. (Designed and woven by Virginia Joy.)

8-13. A back view of the poncho in Figure 8–12.

tern drafts only the picked-up threads of the pattern are shown as they lie on the surface of the background warps. The pattern sheds are not indicated since they automatically form their part of the pattern. Pick-ups are always made on alternate sheds; thus the overlapping pattern warp floats pass over three wefts in all cases. The alternates may be of single warp threads or pairs. The pattern drafts in Figure 8–21 show the way pick-up of pattern warps or pairs of warps is made on alternate rows.

Select two related shades: two greens, blues, or warm colors. Thread the loom so that the first and last four threads are the same color, thus forming a solid edge stripe. Thread the center section of the band with 29 threads (or any uneven number), alternating light and dark across the loom.

Raise the shed that lifts the pattern threads to the surface and weave. Then pick up the center pattern thread and keep it up while you change to the shed bringing up the background threads. (Or you can change shed and pick the center pattern thread up and bring it up to the surface. Find the way that seems fastest and most accurate for you.) Weave.

Raise the pattern shed and weave.

59

Raise the background threads. This time the center thread goes down to the bottom layer with the other pattern threads and the pattern thread on each side is picked or held up. Weave.

Raise the pattern shed and weave.

Repeat these shed changes, making the pick-up according to the pattern shown on the bag and in pattern No. 7 of Figure 8–20. Pick-up will go slowly at first, but soon you will find your own special way to do this technique which people have been doing for more than a thousand years. Keep the tension tight so that the pattern will be firm and even. If the tension is too loose, the pattern won't hold together and will not look right. (For some more complicated pick-up designs, see *Byways in Handweaving* by Mary Meigs Atwater and also *Weaving Inkle Bands* by Harriet Tidball.)

8-14. The wall hanging was made of a single inkle band with pick-up patterns in black and white yarns. (Woven by Hilda Underhill.)

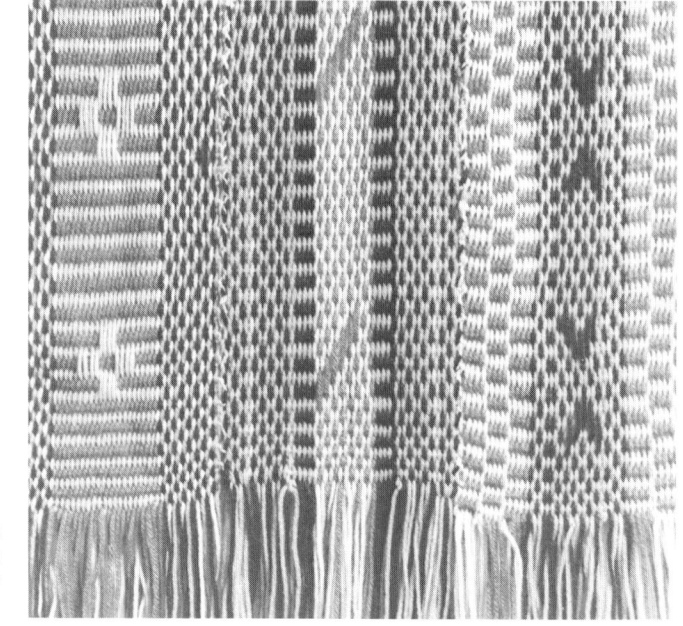

8-15. These inkle bands with various designs were joined together to make a small light-weight afghan. (Woven by Hilda Underhill.)

8-16. A close-up view of a pick-up design for inkle-band weaving is shown. This band was used as a joining for narrow weavings, but could also be used to join machine-woven fabrics. (Woven by Virginia Joy.)

8-17. This inkle band with pick-up design is being used as a valance for linen blinds. (Woven by Virginia Joy.)

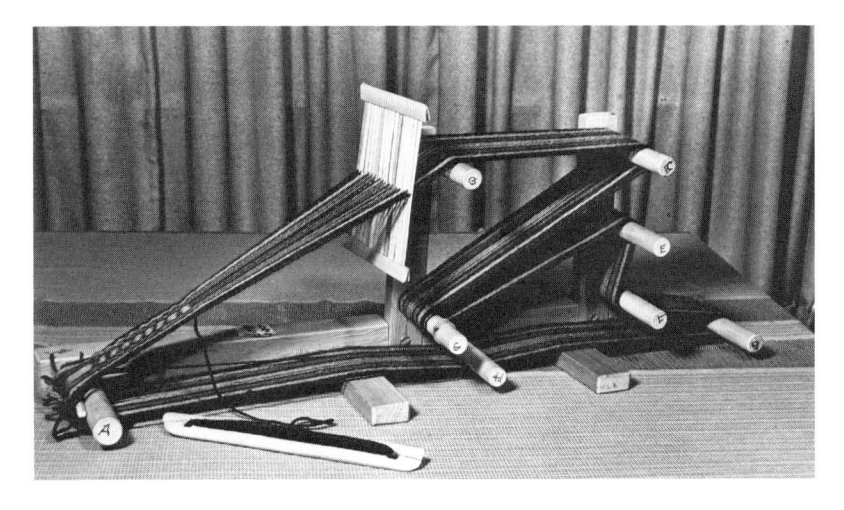

8-18. If an inkle loom is threaded through a rigid heddle rather than with string heddles, the inkle loom can serve as a frame for a backstrap warp.

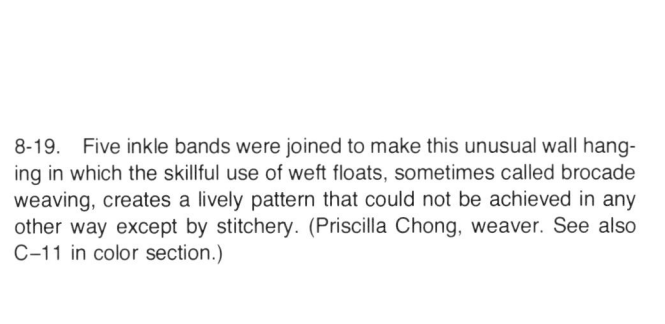

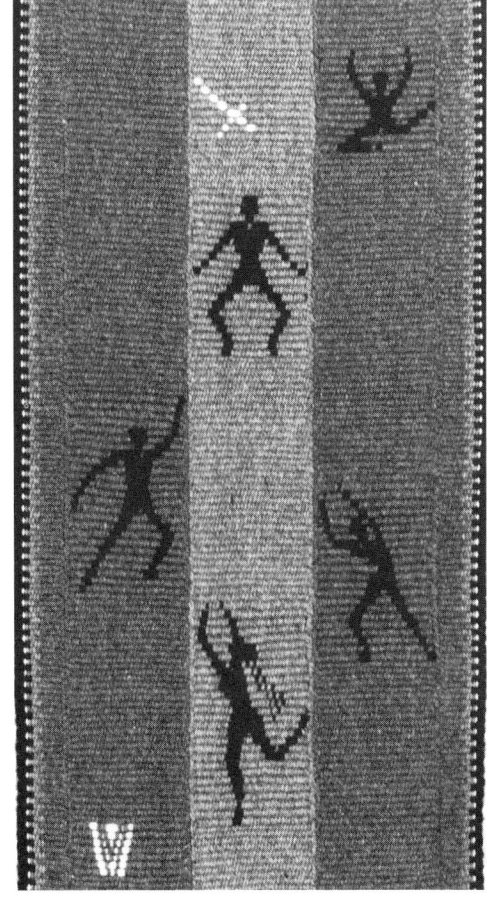

8-19. Five inkle bands were joined to make this unusual wall hanging in which the skillful use of weft floats, sometimes called brocade weaving, creates a lively pattern that could not be achieved in any other way except by stitchery. (Priscilla Chong, weaver. See also C–11 in color section.)

Weft floats can also be used as pattern elements for bands. Usually the pattern weft is a soft yarn, loosely stranded, so it will spread and cover a plain weave band. The supplemental weft is used along with a regular weft and is entered from the wrong side at the point you wish to start the design, on the surface of the band, then carried the required distance on top, then taken back through the warp to the underside at the end of the float. The dense structure of the warp-faced band grips the auxiliary weft firmly; the ends on the wrong side can be clipped closely and left that way without any additional securing.

8-20. These pick-ups were designed by Virginia Joy.

8-21. Corresponding pattern drafts for the pick-up designs in Figure 8–20.

9.
card-woven bands

9-1. Both sides of a card-woven belt made by Mary M. Atwater are shown. (Courtesy of Costume and Textile Study Center, School of Home Economics, University of Washington.)

Today, card weaving is challenging weavers with its possibilities of development into sculptural forms, as well as because of the distinctive belts and trims it produces. The loom is unique, and up to now the fabric woven on it has remained handwoven, as yet untranslated into any commercial, mechanical weaving, since no machine or power loom has been able to duplicate its characteristic twisting.

Although it disappeared and was almost completely forgotten after the Middle Ages, card weaving emerged from time to time in the early nineteenth and twentieth centuries. There was always someone in a remote area who could still remember the technique. Card weaving was introduced in the United States about forty years ago when Mary Meigs Atwater delved into card-weaving patterns and techniques with her acknowledged thoroughness, and examined and analyzed bands from Arabia to Finland, painstakingly recording and representing the examples she found. (See the Bibliography: *Byways in Handweaving*.)

Card-woven bands have a distinct structural characteristic not found in other types of band weaving: a twisted four-ply construction, a form of warp twining, extremely strong in its lengthwise direction. The terms "card weaving" and "tablet weaving" are interchangeable, but in the United States we use the first because the weaving devices are usually made of cardboard and their shape is a little like those of playing cards. They are the heddle arrangement for the weaving and the design in the weaving is achieved by turning the cards and by the color sequence of the threads.

Strong, nonsticky yarns such as perle cotton, double quick crochet cotton, tapestry wool yarns, and linen are good yarns to use at first; however, after you have become accustomed to the weaving technique, you should feel free to use any yarns or combinations of yarns you wish.

You can make your own cards for the loom from stiff cardboard, about cereal-box weight, or you can buy them at

9-2. In this detail of a segment of a three-quarter-inch-wide card-woven band made of perle cotton in four colors, study the twist of the threads and the direction of the threading of the cards.

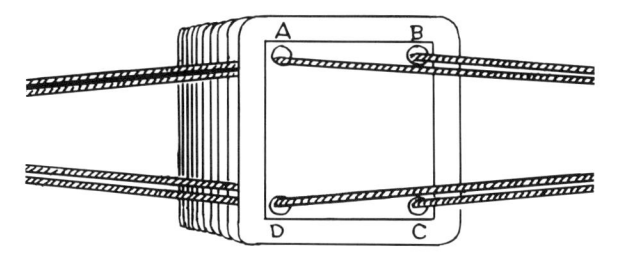

9-3. The cards, lined up parallel to the threads, are ready for weaving.

9-4. The frame of a strong old loom holds long warps under tension for card weaving. Herbi Gray is the weaver.

weaving supply shops. The card should be approximately 3½" square with ⅜" holes set diagonally about 1" from each corner. Threading the cards will be easier if the holes are lettered consecutively, ABCD, clockwise around the card. (Figure 9–3.) Most pattern drafts will be easy to follow if you use this lettering method both for the pattern and the corresponding holes in the cards.

You will also need a small shuttle and some means of holding the threads at tension. To get this tension, you can weave backstrap style, use a hitching post as shown in Figure 3–8 or devise a frame like the stretcher frame in Figure 7–16. If you have a floor or table loom, simply push the heddles aside, remove the beater, and roll the warp onto the back beam, using your loom tension control.

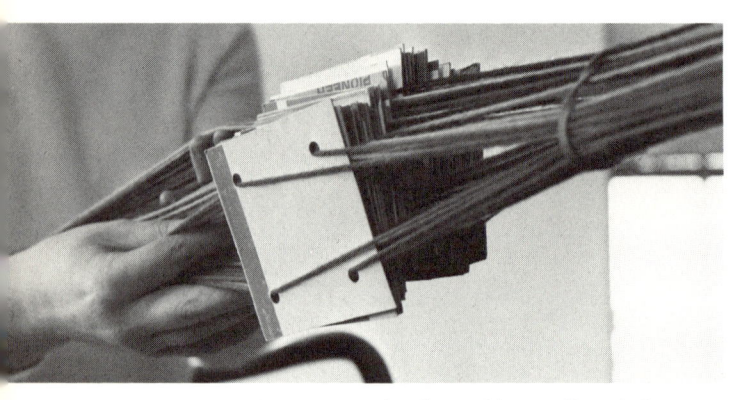

9-5. This set of cards is made of cereal boxes. Rounded corners would have made them smoother to use.

9-6. Three small projects for first-time card-weaving are shown: A bookmark and a watchband made with the pattern described in the text and illustrated in Figures 9–7 and 9–8; and a pair of shoelaces woven by Ellyn Miller in a plain five-card pattern.

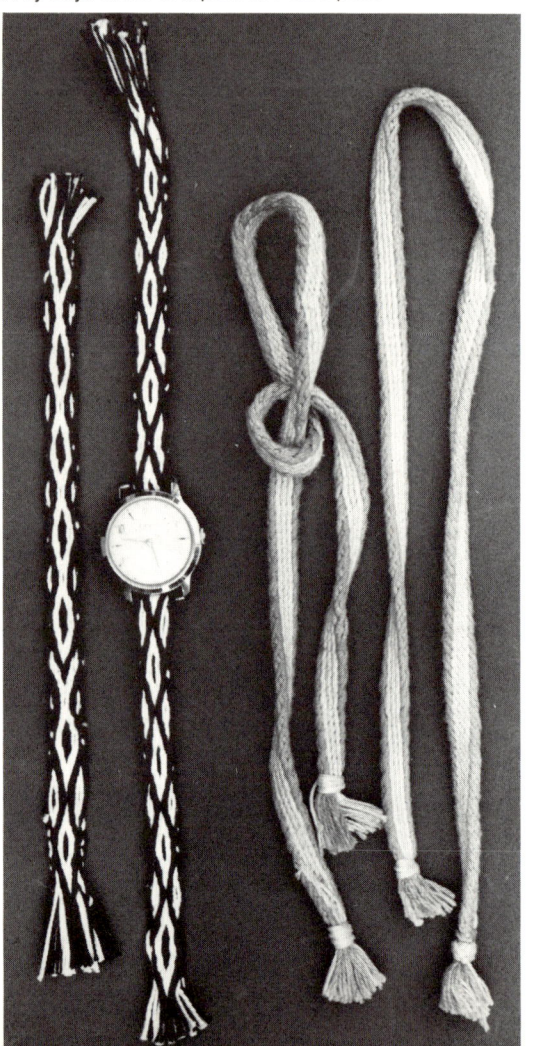

For a first project you will need 10 cards and a short warp of about one and one-half yards of perle cotton No. 5 or crochet cotton of about the same weight. The narrow band you will be weaving can be used as a bookmark, a watchband, a dog collar, or trim for a shirt or a curtain. It could even be used for a belt, although it would be quite a narrow one. (Figure 9–6.)

Look at the detail of the pattern in Figure 9–7. This is a two-color, 10-card pattern for which you will need a total of 24 dark threads and 16 light ones. Measure off the threads in groups of four for each separate card. You may place them in groups of four on a table or work space. It makes threading easier if you keep the threads separated in these groups so they are ready to go in their particular card when you begin warping.

9-7. This design was made by turning the cards four one-quarter turns forward and four turns back.

9-8. With the same threading as for Figure 9–7, this time eight turns forward and eight turns back were used. The main part of the bookmark in Figure 9–6 was made with the four turn sequence, with an experimental weaving at one end.

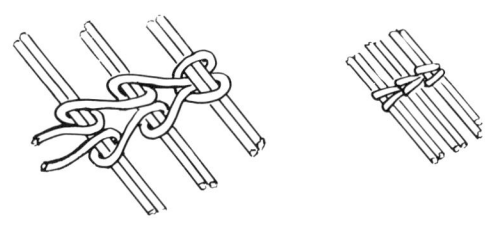

9-9. Chain links keep the groups of threads in order. The drawing at the right shows how the groups of threads look when they lie close together.

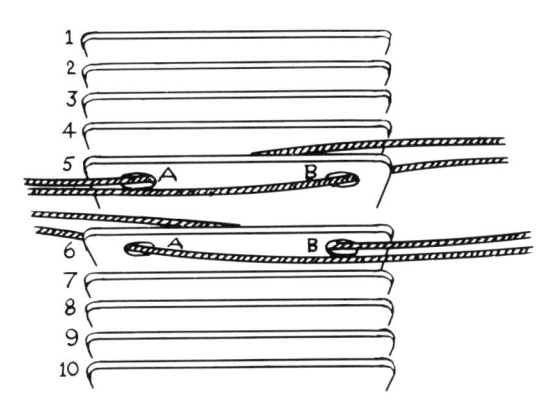

9-10. Card No. 6 has been threaded from front to back and card No. 5 from back to front.

A looped chain such as the one shown in Figure 9–9 works quite well for keeping the groups separated for threading. To make the loop, fold a strand of yarn about 24 " long in half. Start with a lark's head loop (see Figure 3–9), around the first group of threads. Then bring both free ends up and around the next group of threads, through the center space between the chaining yarns, pull down, and repeat the process until all the groups are measured and ready for warping. For longer warps use a warping board or turn a card table upside down and use the upturned legs for measuring.

Measure four dark threads and place the first loop of the chain around these four. Now measure one dark, two light and one dark for the second card and place the second link of the chain around these four. Next, measure two light and two dark threads, separate these with the next loop of the chain, and go to the next four, which will be one light, two dark, and one light. The last group of threads for card No. 5 will be two dark and two light.

You are halfway through now, so you will mirror the procedure, starting with two dark, and two light; next one light, two dark, and one light; then two light and two dark; then one dark, two light, and one dark; and finally four dark.

You are now ready to thread the cards. There are two threading directions for placing the pattern through the holes in the cards. One way to describe the threading system is to instruct you to thread from the *front* of the card or the *back* of the card; the other way is to direct you to thread *up* or *down*. In Figure 9–10 note that the cards can be threaded either from the lettered side or from the blank side — the unlettered side. In writing patterns and giving threading instructions, we will use the terms *back* for the unlettered side and *front* for the lettered side. On some patterns you will find little arrows beneath or above the pattern symbol. These arrows point up for threading from the front and down for threading from the back.

Tie one end of the threads together with a strong cord and if you wish, you can fasten this end to some sort of hitching post, or you can leave the threads spread out on a work surface while you do the warping. Lay the cards, which you have numbered from one to 10 and with No. 10 on top, face up in a stack. Use a pencil to number the cards, because you may want to reuse them with different numbers.

Thread the cards one by one, following the pattern indicated in Figure 9–11. Card No. 10 will have a dark thread in each of the holes and the thread will be inserted from the front to the back of the card (from the lettered side). Card No. 9 will have a dark thread in A, a light one in B, a light one in C, and a dark one in D. Card No. 8 will have a light thread in A and B and a dark one in C and D. Continue to follow the pattern, inserting the threads from the front until you have threaded five cards or are halfway through the pattern.

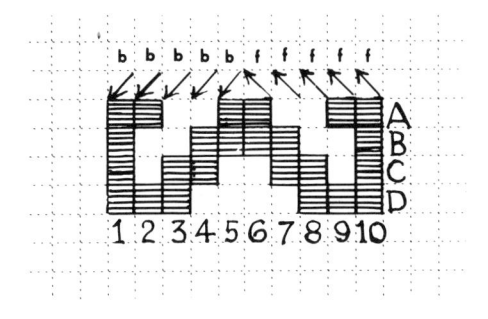

9-11. This pattern draft for threading will yield the band designs shown in Figures 9–6, 9–7, and 9–8.

Now with card No. 5 ready to be threaded, insert a dark thread in A and B and a light thread in C and D. These threads will be placed through the holes from the back of the card (from the blank side). Continue to thread the remaining cards from the back, following the pattern, slipping the chain off each group of four threads and checking the threading direction each time. It will all go slowly at first, but after you've done it once or twice the entire procedure will come easily and quickly to you.

Now wind the weft around a shuttle. Use a belt shuttle or netting shuttle, or even a shuttle you have made yourself out of a strong cardboard. For weft use the same yarn as you are using for warp.

Place a couple of rubber bands around the cards so they won't slip around and get entangled while you put your weaving under tension. (Figure 9–12.) You can tie a cord around the ends you have threaded through the cards and tie this cord around your waist to give tension, or use any of the methods that have been noted before.

Before weaving, make sure you have all the cards facing the same way, with the same lettered edges at the top — either AB, BC, CD or DA. This will be your starting position.

You will make a one-quarter turn of the pack of cards parallel to the threads — that is, from AB to DA, for example. (Figure 9–13.) You can start by turning the cards either away from you or toward you, but make a note of the direction you start, so that you will continue to turn in that direction. You could take a piece of cardboard, draw an arrow on it, and place it beside your weaving area with the arrow pointing in the direction you wish to turn the cards. To keep track of the number of turns you make in one direction, get a number of beans, small stones, or buttons and move one of these from

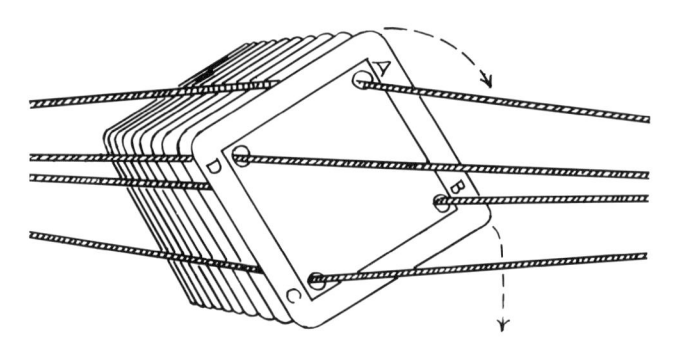

9-13. A quarter turn of the entire pack of cards parallel to the threads creates a new shed, with AD at the top.

9-14. A direction arrow and some counters will help keep track of the turns you make.

9-12. This way the weaving stays in order when you leave it or while it is being transported if you happen to be weaving backstrap style.

the bottom to the top of the arrow as you make each turn. (Figure 9–14.)

Start with four as an arbitrary number of turns and alternate between four quarter turns away from you and four quarter turns toward you until you see the pattern emerging. You may want to think of this as four weft shots. Then do experiment as much as you like; just keep track of the number of turns you make in each direction until you find a pattern that is pleasing to you. For example, you might make two forward and two back, then eight forward and eight back, or four and four with eight and eight.

Be sure to insert one weft shot with each turn of the cards. This turning of the cards is similar to the change in harness position of a loom, so a weft thread is needed each time to hold the threads in place. Hold the cards loosely in your hands; if you tighten up on the cards, the warp threads will stick and a card might not make its turn. To clear the shed for the shuttle, slide the pack of cards up and down the warp once or twice and the threads will separate.

If the pattern seems to be off, check the top corner of the cards to be certain they all show the same letter. Sometimes the pattern will be on the reverse side of your band, but this means you have set the cards up so that the weaving is upside down. It won't matter as long as you keep accurate track of the turns of the cards.

Because the tension increases rapidly with this method of band weaving, watch it closely and loosen it as soon as you see that your band is not keeping its shape and pattern. Check the general band weaving instructions in Chapter 2 for instructions on how to keep to the correct width, start and finish of your band, and avoid uneven edges.

The shoelaces in Figure 9–6 might be a good summer camp project for which you need only 5 cards and 3 colors of carpet warp or crochet cotton. Measure and cut enough yarn for each pair of shoelaces; fifty-four inches will give you two laces of from 21″ to 23″ long.

Measure 4 strands of pink, 4 strands of yellow, 4 strands of blue, and 4 each of yellow and pink. (Use other colors if you prefer; these are only suggestions.)

Thread card No. 1 with all pink (in holes ABC and D), card No. 2 with all yellow, card No. 3 with all blue, card No. 4 with all yellow and card No. 5 with all pink. Thread all the cards in the same direction.

Tie both ends of the warp as explained in the first project and weave by turning the cards 4 turns forward and 4 backward (away from you and toward you) or any combinations

9-15. A more advanced card-weaving project.

69

you wish to use. There will be no pattern — just stripes and a strong handwoven band. When you have finished weaving the shoelaces, cut them from the loom and bind the ends with sewing thread to make a stiff end for lacing through the grommets in shoes.

If you have been card weaving for a while, you might like to try making the belt in Figure 9-15. The threading pattern is No. 10 in Figure 9-28. (See also the first belt in C-17 of the color section.)

You will need 40 strands of navy blue thread, 24 strands of white, and 16 strands of red. White thread will also be used for the weft. Measure and cut an ample amount of warp for your belt — allow one-third more yarn than the finished band.

Follow the threading directions for the pattern in the tenth draft of Figure 9-28. (In these drafts we just use the letters "b" and "f" to tell you to thread from the front or the back of the cards, since the arrows confuse some people and are not really needed. We used the arrows in Figure 9-11 to show how they would look in some of the books that use them.) Set the warp up under tension, and weave with four turns away from you and four turns back toward you. Weave for about four inches, or a given number of patterns. (The four turns away and four toward you make one pattern.)

Now lift the first six and the last six cards up with both hands (Figure 9-16) and place them in the center of the band, thus splitting the red and white section in half. You will now have twelve blue and white cards in the center and four red and white cards on each side, whereas before you had six blue and white cards on each side and a red and white center section of eight cards.

Weave again for a given number of patterns; then lift the center section out again with both hands, six cards in each hand, place these two sections outside the red and white section, and leave the latter in the middle once more. Then just continue weaving the band.

There are an infinite number of ways you can use this card weaving procedure. You could apply it to your less functional weaving to create intriguing effects in wall hangings or in weaving that you could wear. It is a braided effect that is difficult to obtain with ordinary looms.

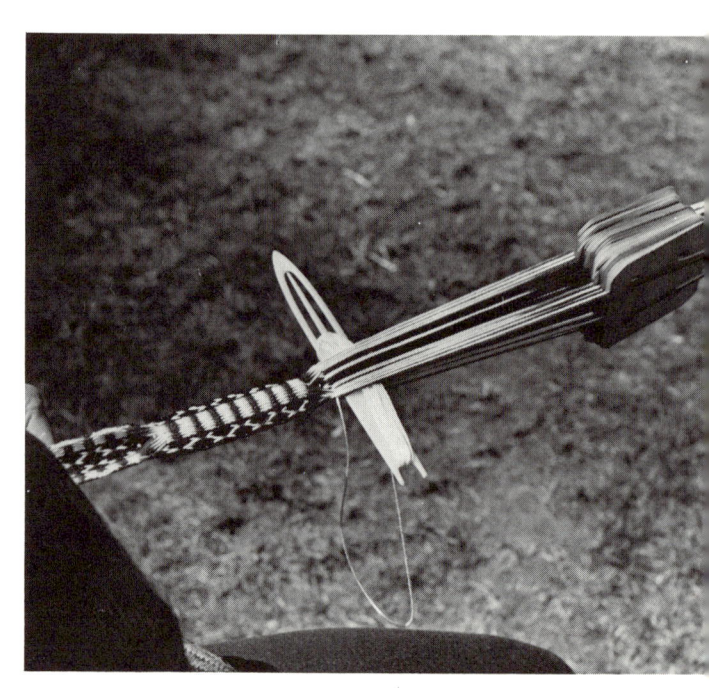

9-17. Back to the original pattern, with the red and white striped section in the center.

Another interesting variation to try is Icelandic double weave, which is not the four-ply twisted weave of the traditional card-woven fabric, but rather a two-surface weave that sandwiches some of the warp threads in between the two

9-16. The blue and white sections of each side now come to the center.

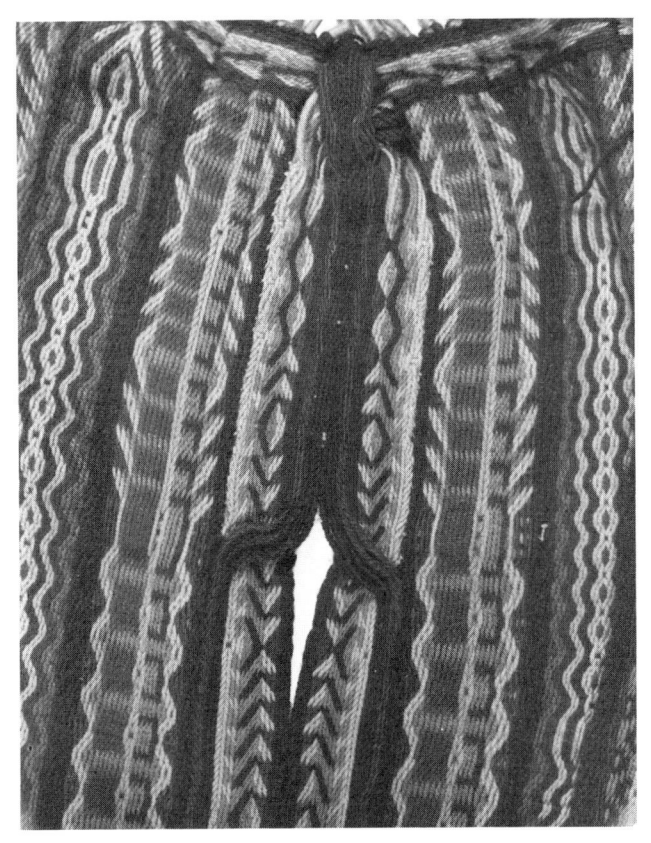

9-18. In this back section of a cape constructed from card-woven strips, note the center section, where the cards were lifted and replaced in the same manner as was described in Figure 9–16. (Woven by Candace Crockett.)

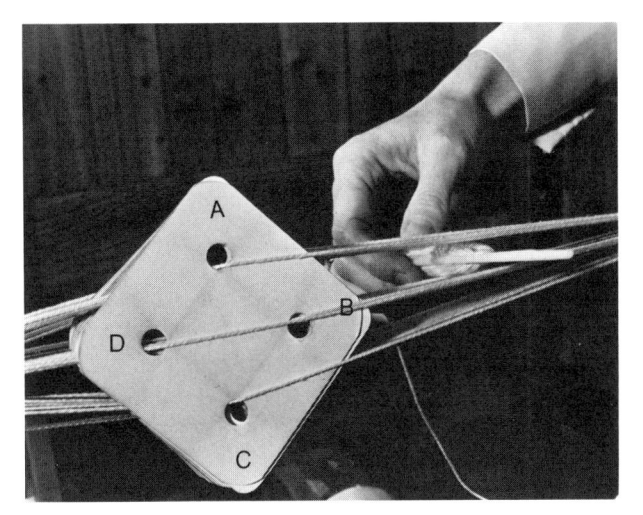

9-19. Icelandic double weave.

will weave the center section of warp and leave the top and bottom sections unwoven.

Herbi Gray has developed a design she calls "window weaving" as a result of a happy error made by her six-year-

9-20. Herbi Gray's individual "window-woven" bands were mounted on Plexiglas for hanging.

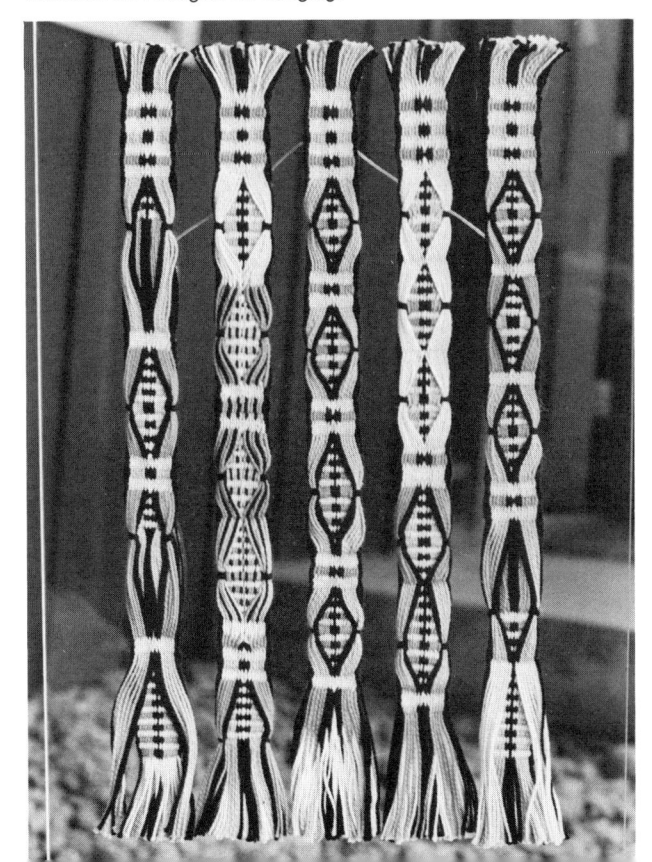

woven surfaces. For this weave you turn the cards one-eighth turn for the first shed so that only one corner is up. For example, if you use the AB side of the card, turn it so that just the A corner is up. (Figure 9–19.) This will make two sheds, with a section of warp threads in between; these warp threads will remain unwoven. Carry the weft first through the top shed and then back through the lower shed. Next, turn the B corner up, pass the weft through the upper and lower sheds once more, then turn back to the A corner and repeat these two shed changes as long as you wish, making certain that you insert the weft from right to left through the top shed and then from left to right through the lower shed before each turning of the cards.

By turning the cards one quarter turn from AB to BC, then back to AB, then to BC, repeating only these two turns, you old daughter Joey when she was learning to do card weaving. (Figures 9–20 and 9–21.) Instead of turning the cards the one-quarter turn from one side to the next to make four turns, the little girl simply turned the cards one-quarter turn away from her and one-quarter turn toward her, so that only the middle was woven and the warps on the top and bottom remained unwoven. Seeing the possibilities there, her mother pulled those unwoven warps to either side, caught them there and made "window weaving."

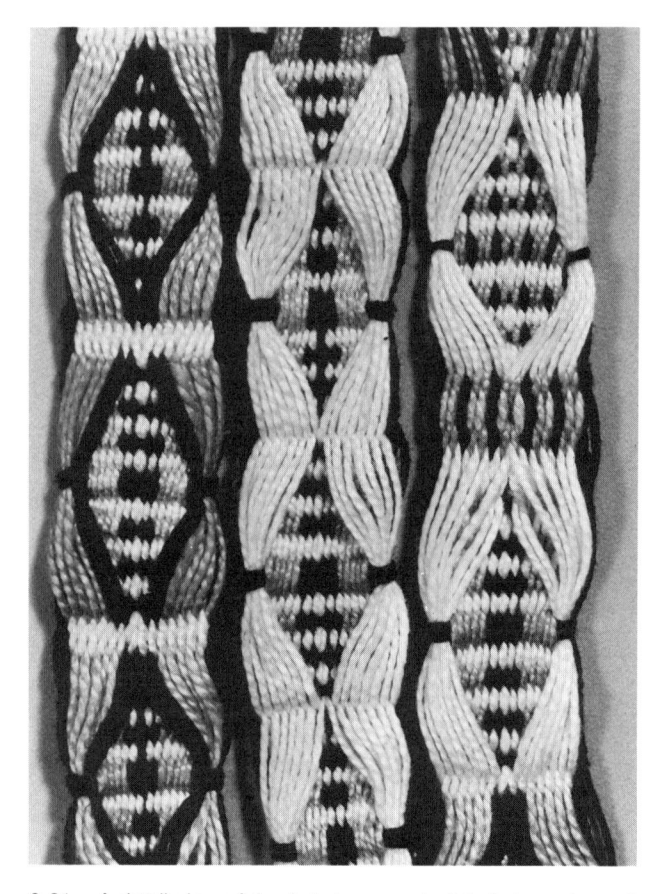

9-21. A detail view of the "window weaving" technique shown in Figure 9–20. This kind of weaving could be expanded into large sculptural forms.

9-22. Three wooden beads add a smart finishing touch to a simple black and white card-woven belt. (A student work under the direction of Louise Williams.)

9-23. Bellpulls made of card-woven bands could be an easy beginning project in which you can use your leftover practice bands. (Designed and woven by Herbi Gray.)

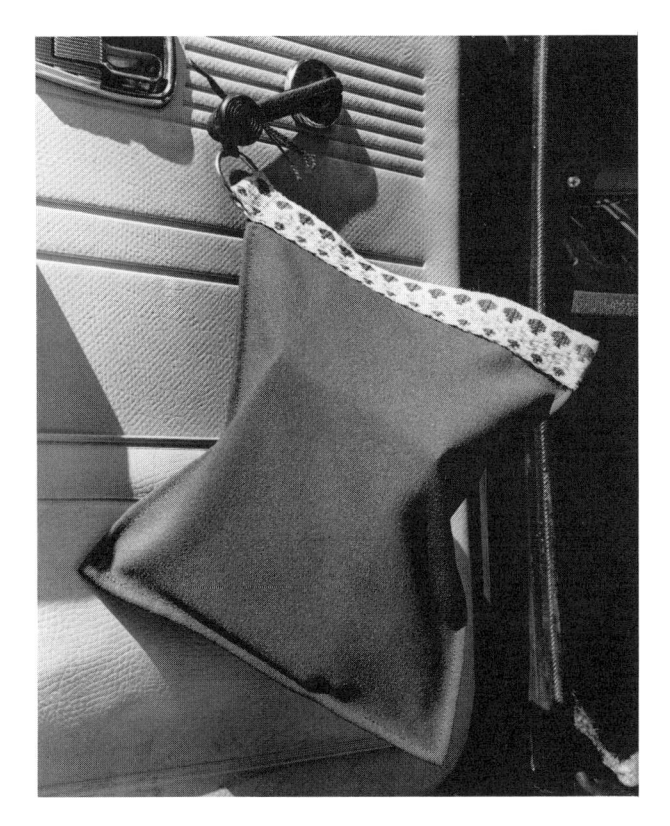

9-24. A litter bag is edged with a card-woven band designed by Herbi Gray, who used green trees and blue water as her inspiration.

9-25. A close-up view of the band design in Figure 9–24 shows the tree and water shapes.

Another experimental weaving procedure in card weaving is to turn the cards a number of times without using a weft. This gives a twist to four threads at a time and is again an effect that could be developed and incorporated into wall hangings or decorative trim as well as belts.

Card-woven bands may be woven along with a four-harness fabric to make a finished edge for a pillow, or, as in Figure 9–26, a pad for a weaving bench. Many card-weaving designs adapt to four-harness weaving in such a way as to expand the size of the band. The napkin rings in Figure 9–27 are about 2½" wide and were woven on a four-harness loom.

9-26. Weaving a card-woven band along with a four-harness fabric.

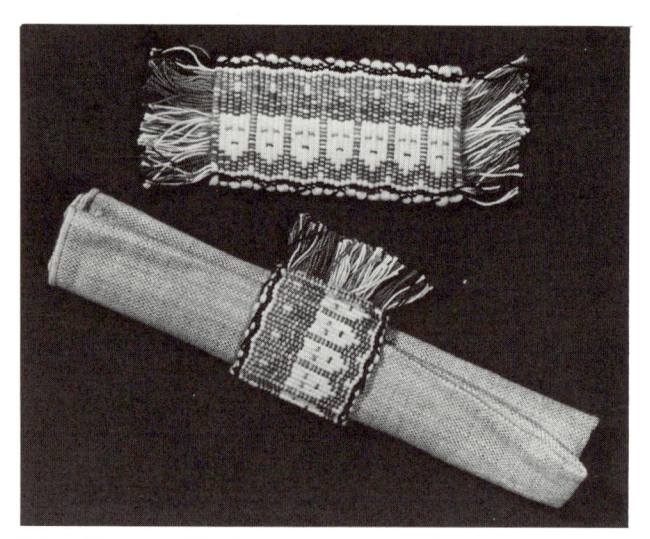

9-27. These napkin rings were woven by Ethel Jackson from a design that appeared in the *Pinella Guild Bulletin* for December 1965.

9-28. These pattern drafts were designed by Herbi Gray for the card-woven bands in Figure C-18 of the color section.

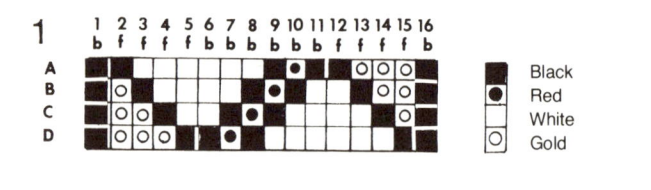

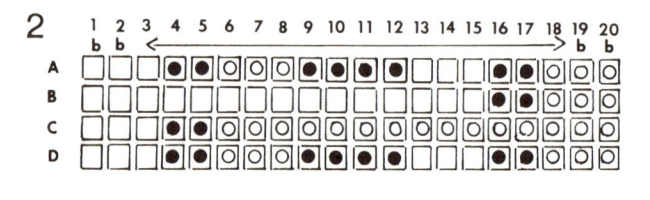

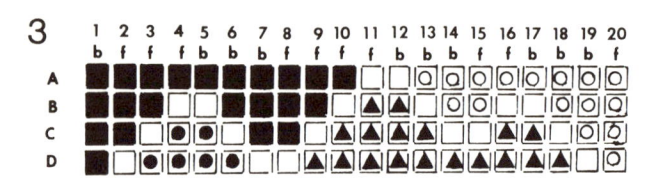

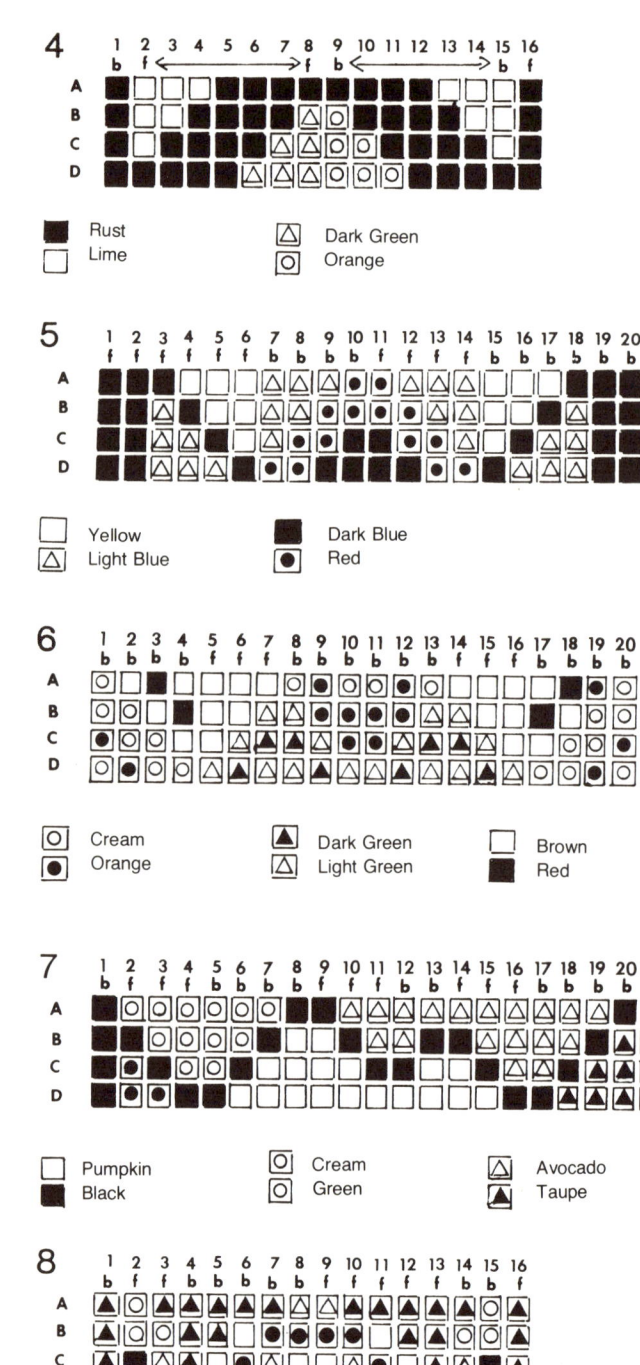

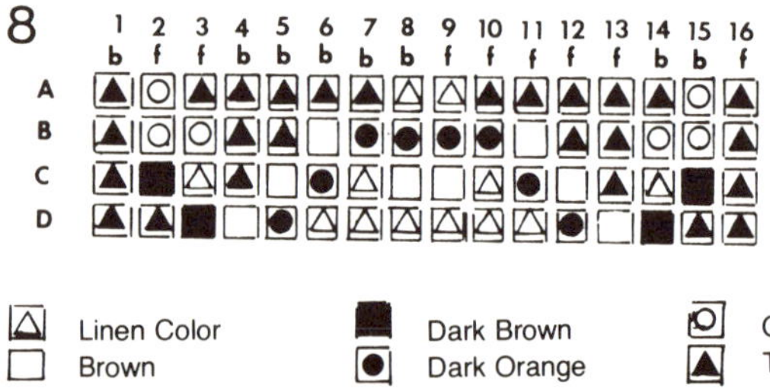

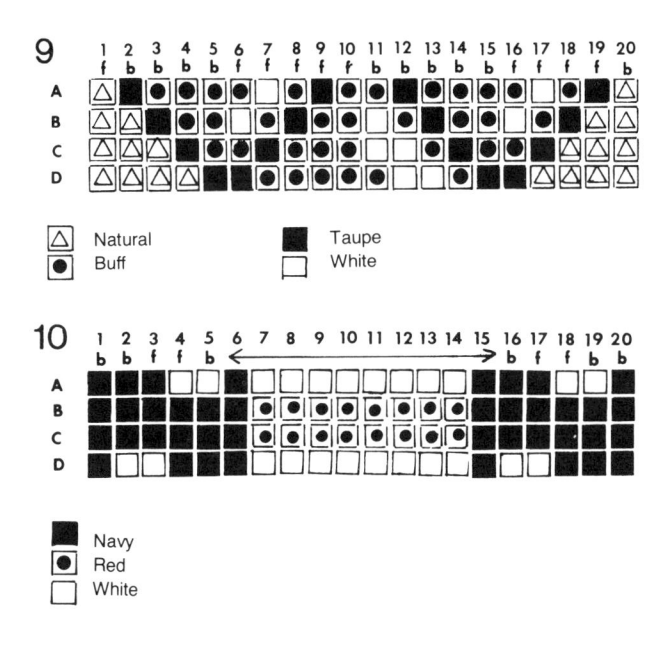

Figure 9–29 shows some more possibilities for design variations. The first band shows a section that was woven without weft. Where the belt seems to spread out, the cards were turned but no weft was used. Belt No. 6 was woven with one weft; then three wefts were used to weave three separate sections and then back to one weft after the twist was made. The seventh is a braided belt that was woven with the addition of strands at the back to widen it; two pins have been placed in the belt to indicate where the strands are added. The eighth belt has a Neolithic design and was woven with the same type of grass that might have been used in 5000 B.C. In the last belt, which was woven with plastic and metallic thread, the cards were all turned the same direction throughout the weaving, thus giving a contour to its shape.

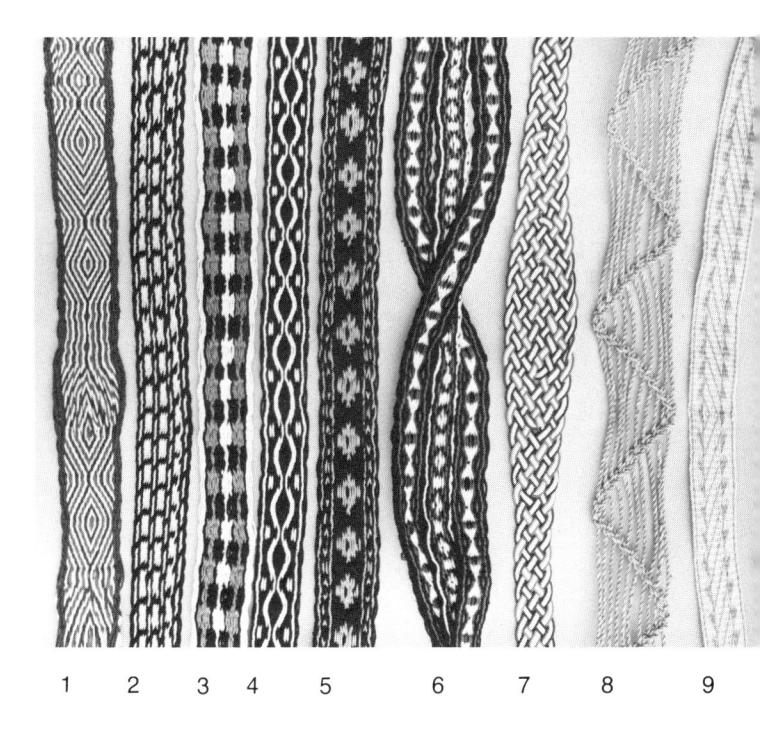

9-29. Belts 3 through 6 were woven by Pat and Ellyn Miller and follow designs from *Card Weaving* by Russell Groff. The last three belts are from the collection of Evelyn Jenkins.

9-30. Pattern drafts for belt Nos. 4 and 6 in Figure 9–29. (Reproduced with permission from *Card Weaving* by Russell Groff.)

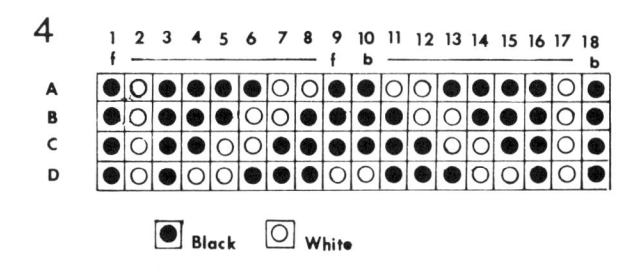

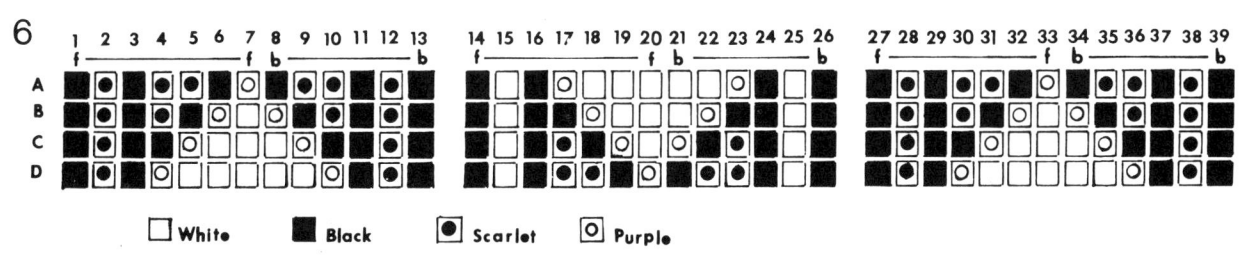

75

10. weaving variations for special effects

Perhaps some of the most provocative effects in band weaving are due to the variations you can make in the weaving processes. For example, you can make buttonholes or slits, wrap sections of the warp threads, add fringe to the sides or at intervals across the width of the band, and add any number and kinds of weft insertions for variety.

Figure C-19 in the color section shows how slits can be used to give added interest to a wall hanging. To weave a slit or buttonhole, you must prepare two wefts. You can make butterflies, wind two shuttles, or use two bobbins. (Figure 10–1.)

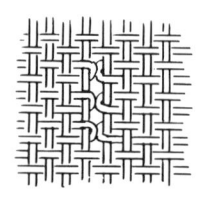

10-1. The left drawing illustrates a slit made between two warps; the right drawing shows how to leave some warps which can be wrapped if you wish.

10-2. Silver buttons were sewn to one end of this Osage-braided belt. The loops formed by braiding and wrapping the fringed ends make excellent buttonholes. (Student work under the guidance of Bill Holm.)

Weave the band with one weft until you are ready to start the slit. Weave one half of the slit with the first weft, then weave the other half of the slit with the other weft. When the slit or buttonhole is long enough, drop the second weft; clip it off with a short tail which you can weave in along with the first weft which continues the band until another slit is needed.

A band may be buttoned on a garment when it isn't practical to sew it on — for example, on a suede or leather coat. Wrapping sections of warp threads and leaving some unwoven are two more ways to add interest to your weaving. You can wrap the warps as you weave while the band is under tension or leave the warps unwoven and wrap them after the band has been taken off the loom.

Figure 10–3 shows you the method for making a wrapped warp or fringe. You place a short length of the wrapping thread from top to bottom along the warps to be wrapped.

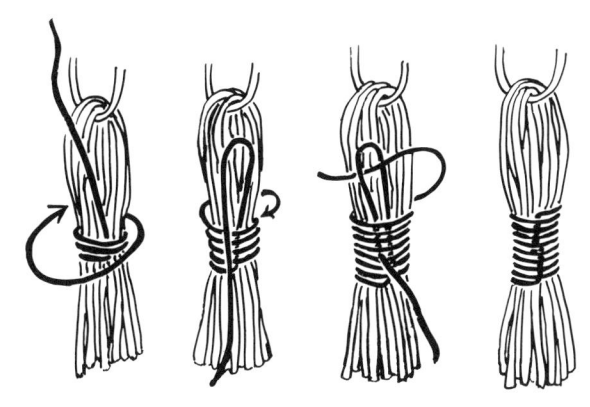

10-3. Wrapping warps or fringes.

10-4. Helen Pope's belt, which she wove of DMC floss, demonstrates a skillful use of wrapped and unwoven warp threads.

10-5. A Guatemalan woven band displays a distinctive wrapped and fringe finish. (Courtesy of the Costume and Textile Study Center, School of Home Economics, University of Washington.)

The wrapping thread should be ample for the space to be wrapped but experience will have to help you gauge your own needs and designs. The length of thread you place along the warps should be a little longer than the area to be wrapped and should stick out above the spot where you will finish wrapping.

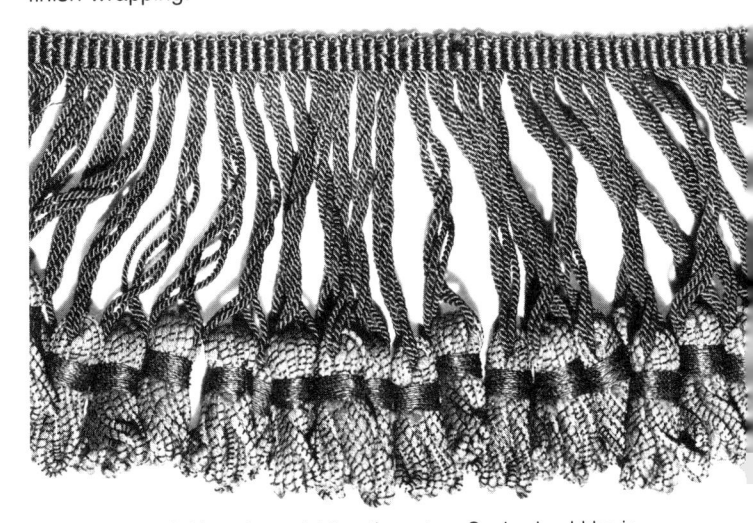

10-6. This weft fringe from eighteenth-century Spain should be inspiring to contemporary weavers. (Courtesy of the Costume and Textile Study Center, School of Home Economics, University of Washington.)

10-7. This woven band has weft fringes. (Courtesy of the Costume and Textile Study Center, School of Home Economics, University of Washington.)

Commence wrapping from the bottom to the top and pull the wrapping cord tight each time, keeping the pull consistent and the threads close together so that you completely cover the warps. When you are near the end of the wrapping, loop the free end down, lapping it over the wrapped area a little way. Then put on another three or four wrapped turns and pass the working end of the cord through the little loop as shown in the drawing. Pull the projecting end to draw both parts under the wraps and then cut off the surplus ends.

Generally in band weaving the weft doesn't need to have strength; it merely lies in each shed holding the warp threads in place to make the pattern and to keep the warps together. Weft insertions, therefore, can be varied to suit the design idea you are trying to achieve. You can use matchsticks, dowels, fringes, Ghiordes knots, unspun wool, or alternating thick and thin wefts.

10-8. Some unusual ideas for weft insertions are shown in these bands woven by Louise Williams.

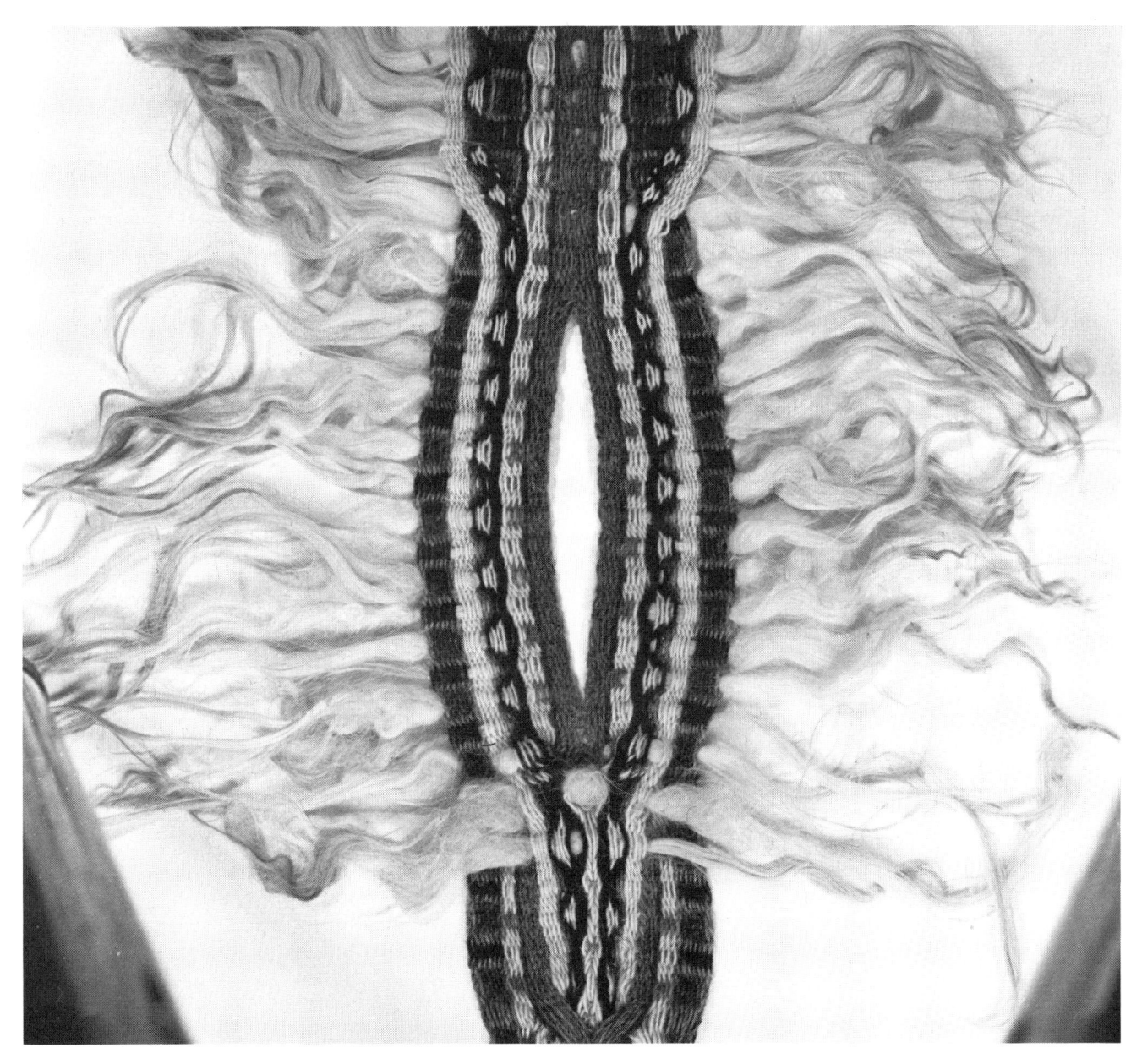

10-9. The center section of the card-woven neckpiece was made of wool with weft insertions and inlays of natural fleece. (Woven by Candace Crockett.)

10-10. A Phillipine skirt shows an ingenious use of fringed trim, which was a laid-in addition to the weft in the band. (Courtesy of Fred and Leslie Hart.)

10-11. The wool tapestry apron is decorated with bands, braids, and fringes. (Of Yugoslavian origin, courtesy of the Costume and Textile Study Center, School of Home Economics, University of Washington.)

10-12. In an imaginative use of inkle weaving created by Thurid Clark, a single band woven of handspun and unspun wools, with fringed insertions and additions of tiny carved seeds, was folded in half to form this striking weed bag and wall hanging.

10-13. The Christmas card "tree" is a woven band with skipped weft areas occupied by 3/8" dowels. Small strips of double-stick tape or glass-head pins will hold the band to the walls while you hang the cards.

10-14. This delicate band used in nineteenth-century France shows weft insertion as well as braided overlay. (Courtesy of the Costume and Textile Study Center, School of Home Economics, University of Washington.)

10-15. Multicolored inkle bands that were woven with knotted fringe weft insertions transform a brocade bedspread into an heirloom. (Woven by Joy Krig.)

To weave a fringe on the side of the band, it is better to use two wefts, one to hold the band in shape and the other to form the fringe. If it is important that all fringe ends be of the same length, make a gauge card that is the desired length of stiff cardboard, hold this card along the side of the band, and carry each weft fringe passage around the card.

Taking the idea of the weft fringe even farther, we go back to the ancient Greek warp-weighted loom. Set up the band warps on your rigid heddle, inkle, or card loom. Again, use two wefts — one to make the band selvedges and the other to stretch out to make a new warp. Instead of weaving vertically and hanging rocks on the wefts that become warps (see Figure 5–4), use a warping board, an upturned table, or a board with nails sticking up at intervals to serve as a measure and a post around which to loop the long wefts.

After the band has been woven, the long wefts become warps for macramé, sprang, or tapestries. (Figure 10–16.) You can mount the band to the top of a frame and secure the warp threads to the bottom. Use nails or tie each warp around the bottom of the frame — use any method that puts the warps under tension for a tapestry or for sprang. For macramé, the warps can hang free for easy knotting.

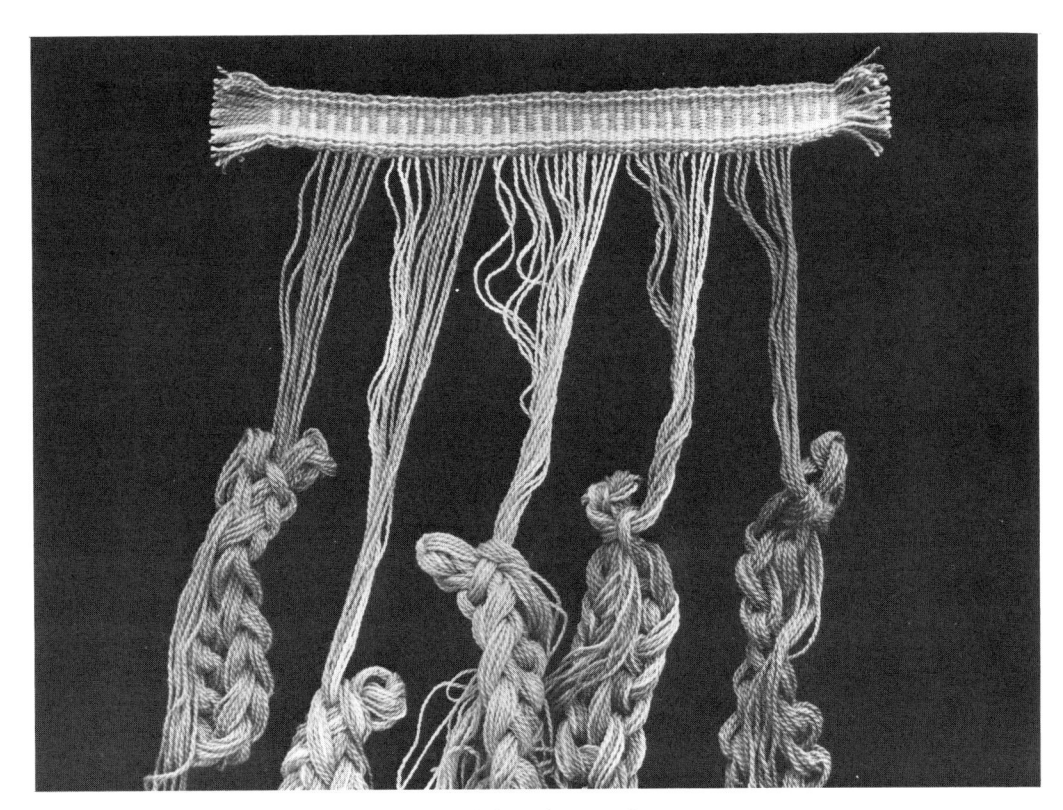

10-16. The woven band's extended weft threads have become the warp threads for the hanging.

Peter Collingwood set up an auxiliary band on cards next to his finished rug and wove the warp ends along with a separate weft to make a rug finish. (Figure 10-17.)

You can use a Ghiordes knot to make pile rugs, fringes, or decorative additions to any weaving. Figure 10-18 shows how to tie the knot around a group of two threads. Always make at least one weft shot above and below each row of knots to hold them in the band. You can also tie Ghiordes knots on the sides of the band.

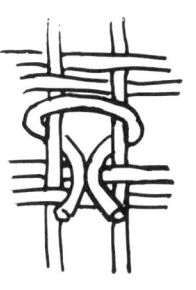

10-17. The card-woven finish of this rug terminates in a tubular weave. (Woven by Peter Collingwood.)

10-18

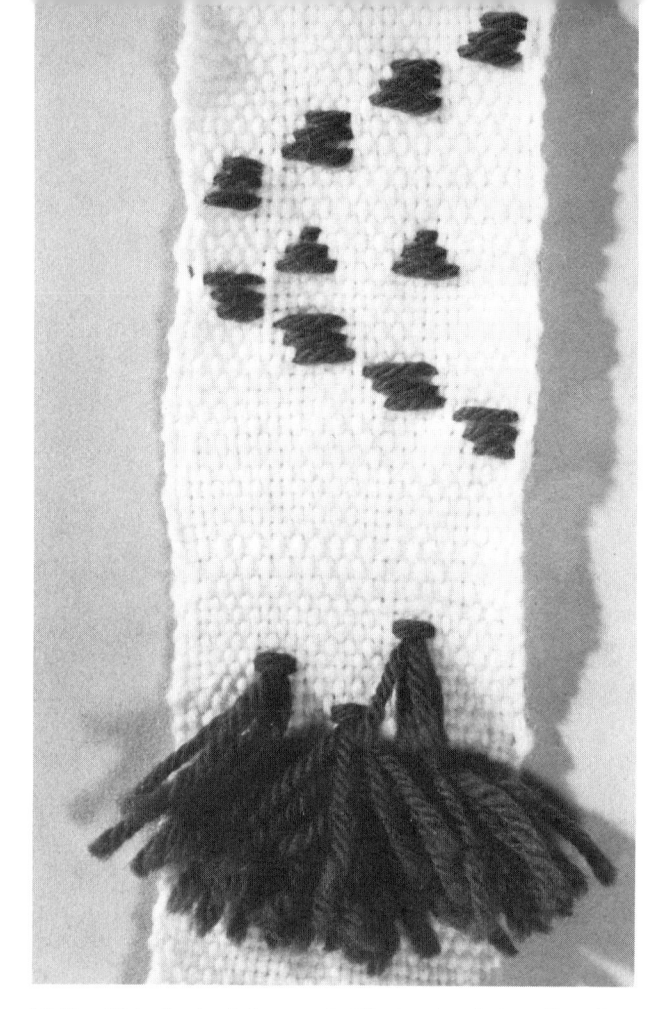

10-19. Ghiordes knots form part of the band and above them is an example of simple weft floats.

When it comes to designing your bands, not only the materials, but the looms themselves will guide you in planning your design. You are not so much limited by your tools as you are influenced by them. Once you are acquainted and comfortable with your tools, you will no longer be conscious of them and then you can begin to let them work for you and express for you the ideas you have been collecting and storing. Some designs will evolve from the combination of band weaving and finger weaving or braiding; others will come about through the manipulation of the devices themselves.

The texture and surface elements of your band can be provocative and interesting design components, particularly when you have begun to weave nonfunctional objects. This does not mean, however, that garments and household accessories should be denied the engaging qualities provided by decorative and innovative ideas.

10-20. In this skillfully designed and meticulously woven inkle-band bag, the yarns are vegetable dyed handspun wools. One long band makes the center and handle for the bag, while two shorter bands are used for the two sides. Functional simplicity was achieved by the weaver, Phoebe McAfee.

10-21. Fringes and decorative shells add an original touch to this shoulder bag made of joined inkle bands. (Woven by Lucy Manz.)

10-22. The woven "man-bag" from Mexico has a partly braided adjustable band as a shoulder strap. (Courtesy of Fred and Leslie Hart.)

10-23. This bag, also from Mexico, was made of joined bands that show a pick-up design. (Courtesy of Alice Carle.)

10-24. Lapped seams join the strips in the inkle-band poncho woven by Barbara Cade, who used natural wools in a white-on-white design.

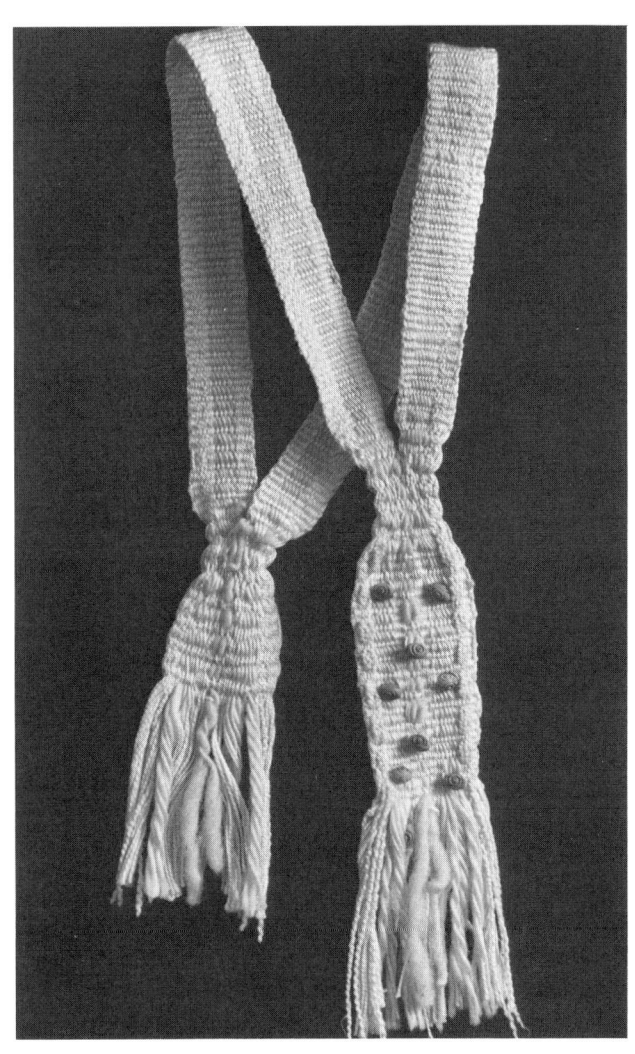

10-25. A skillfully handled idea is demonstrated by this split inkle band which forms a unique necklace of linen, wool, and novelty yarns in off-white. (Woven by Adel Cole.)

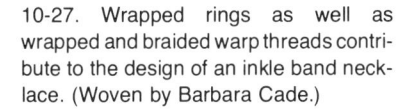

10-26. To make this wool scarf Ann Hinken joined three inkle bands with a crocheted chain.

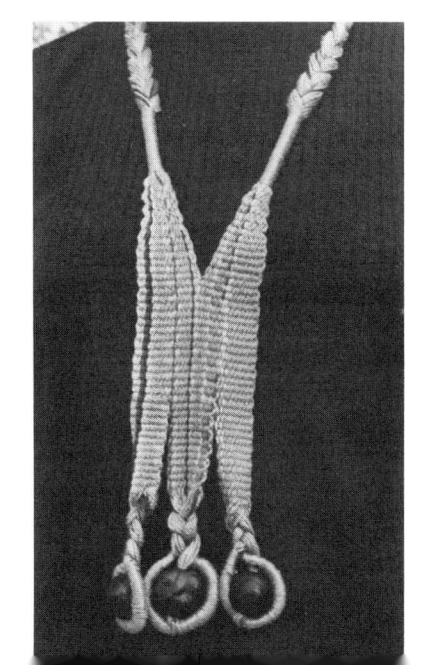

10-27. Wrapped rings as well as wrapped and braided warp threads contribute to the design of an inkle band necklace. (Woven by Barbara Cade.)

87

10-28 and 10-29. In the two jackets from Nepal, the woven bands determine size: The white jacket above has three bands and the brown jacket at right has two. (Courtesy of Mr. and Mrs. Paul Thomas.)

10-30. Gail Bauer wove inkle bands for summer sandals.

10-31. Inkle bands of various designs and materials add color and originality to a long evening skirt. (The bands were woven by Joy Krig.)

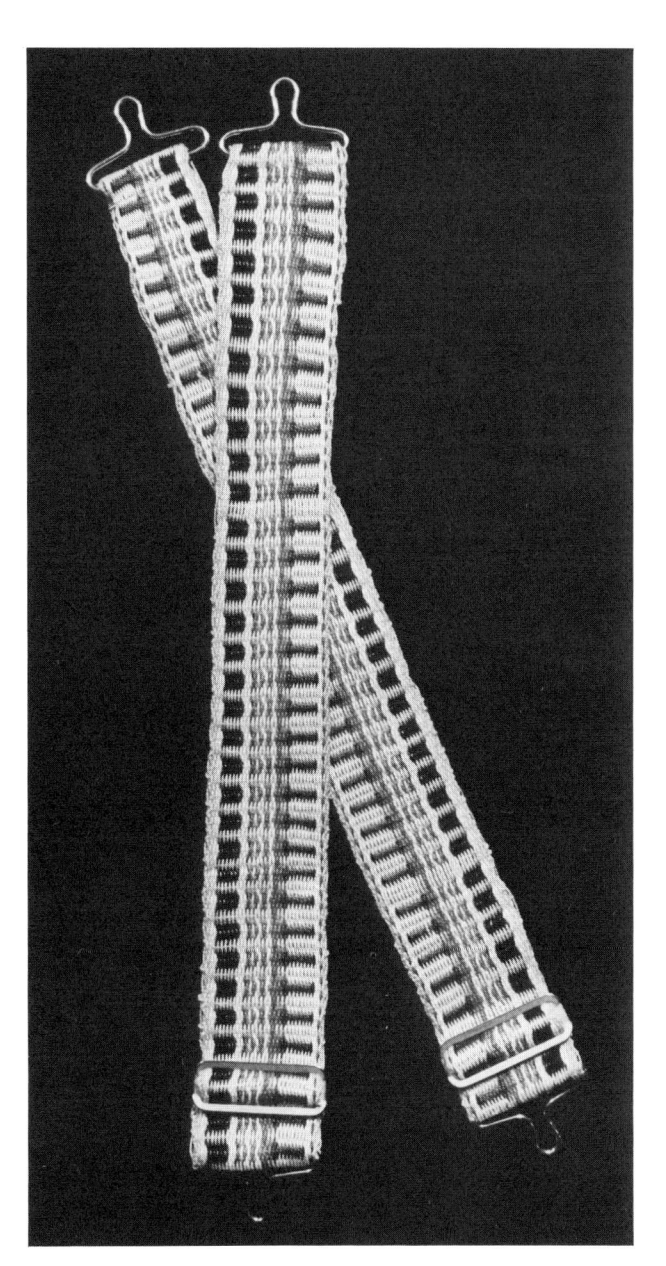

10-32. Louise Williams wove little inkle-band suspenders for her two-year-old son.

89

Just as texture and surface treatment are essential qualities for pleasing design, so is color another vital element. You should consider the sequence, the juxtapositions, and the movement of color within your weaving. The beginner immediately wants to know what colors to put together and how many. But we say, first of all trust your instinct; you know what colors appeal to you and that is not a bad guide. Look to nature's rich variety of colors for inspiration. Examine small details of a single leaf, a single flower, or the underside of a sea-washed stone, for example. Tree bark and twigs also have subtle combinations of color, as do grains of sand. (See Figure C-21 in the color section.) Photographs, paintings, and other of man's works can also be your guides to color use.

Even within the limited construction of the woven band, you, the weaver, can become an artist when you begin to merge your skilled manipulation of materials with the imaginative forces of your mind. Here lies the difference between carefully, meticulously copying and giving form to an original thought. If there is harmony and a response between you and your materials, you will be able to reveal to others the something in you which is unique, which is original. When you are comfortable with the simple looms that have been described in this book, let yourself try new materials, move in new directions, and add new dimensions to your weaving. Prod your imagination and experiment with new surfaces, new contrasts, color concepts, and utilizations of woven bands.

10-33. A rigid heddle band edges a coverlet made of handspun wool.

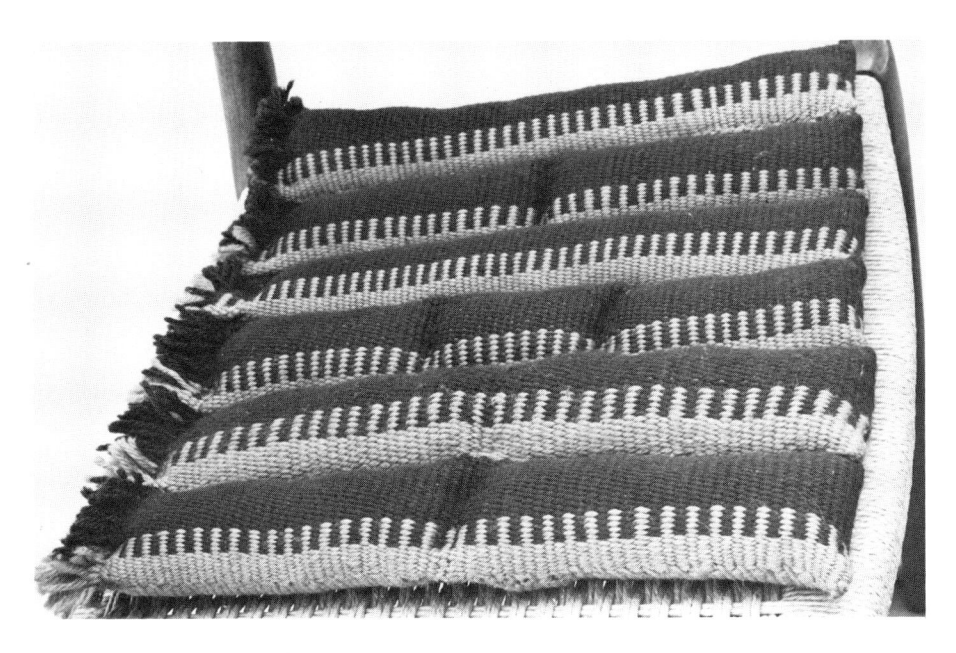

10-34. Folded, stuffed rigid heddle bands have been joined to make a chair pad.

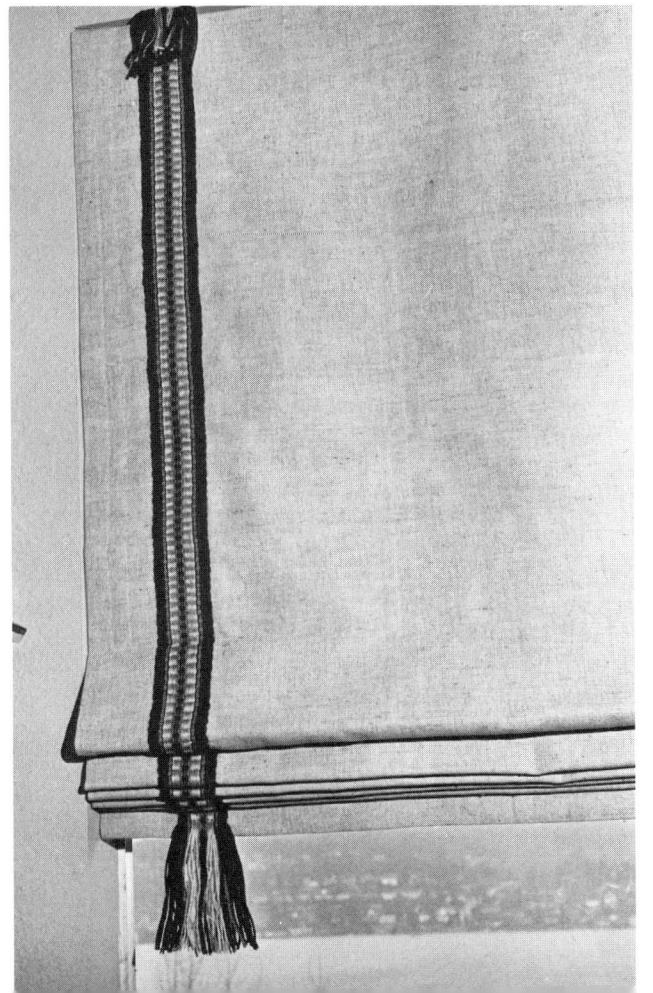

10-36. A wide rigid heddle band seals and conceals the edges of a floor pillow.

10-35. The addition of woven bands lends originality to woven-linen Roman blinds. (Courtesy of Mrs. Cyrus Dimmick.)

10-37. An Equadorian leather hassock is handsomely decorated with a woven band. (Courtesy of Handweaver and Craftsman.)

10-38. The canvas log-carrier uses four-harness woven bands as carrying straps.

10-39. Stuffed bands which have created two whimsical dolls testify to the band-weaver's inspiration. (Woven by Inge Buley.)

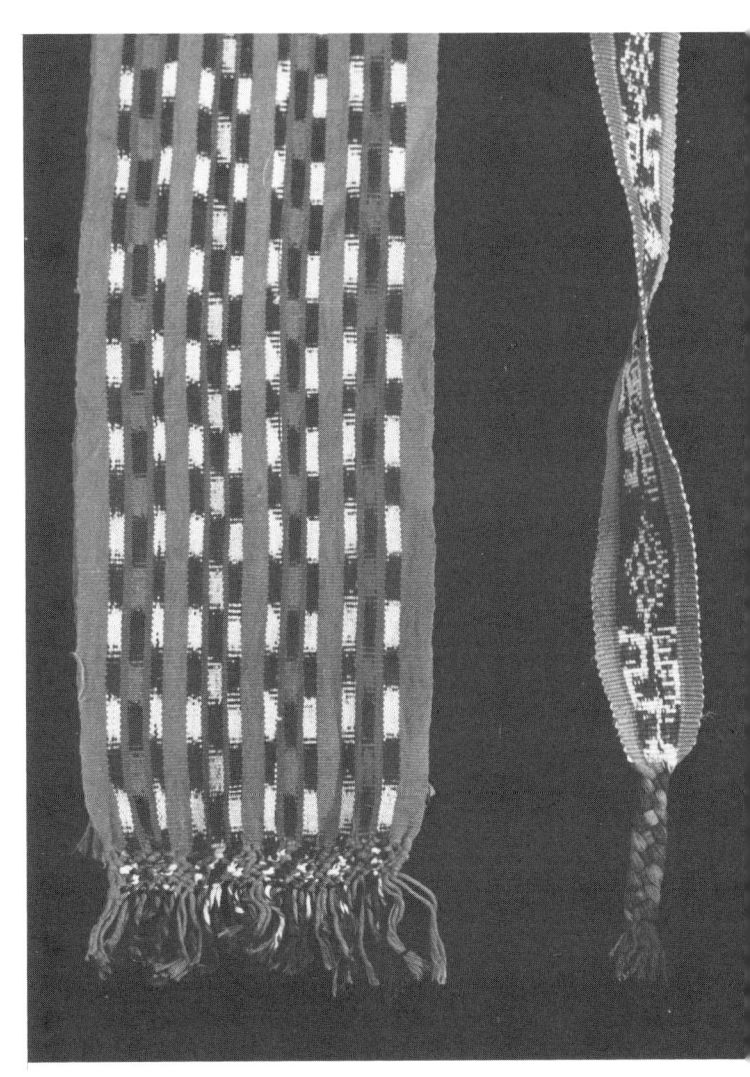

10-40. Guatemalan weaving is a fruitful source for design ideas; Ikat or tie-dyed warps were used for these belts. (The belt on the right is from the collection of Fred and Leslie Hart, and the sash on the left courtesy of the Weaver's Shed.)

93

10-41. A contemporary belt woven by Helen Pope of DMC floss features painted warps that have been carried into the fringes. The unwoven warps can be painted while they are under tension and then they will display the design in a muted way in the finished weaving.

10-42. *Facing page:* This is the kind of design that can occur when the cards are threaded from one direction only. Note the finger-woven braided finish on the fringed end of the card-woven belt. (Woven by Harriet Tidball; from the Tidball collection, courtesy of the Costume and Textile Study Center, School of Home Economics, University of Washington.)

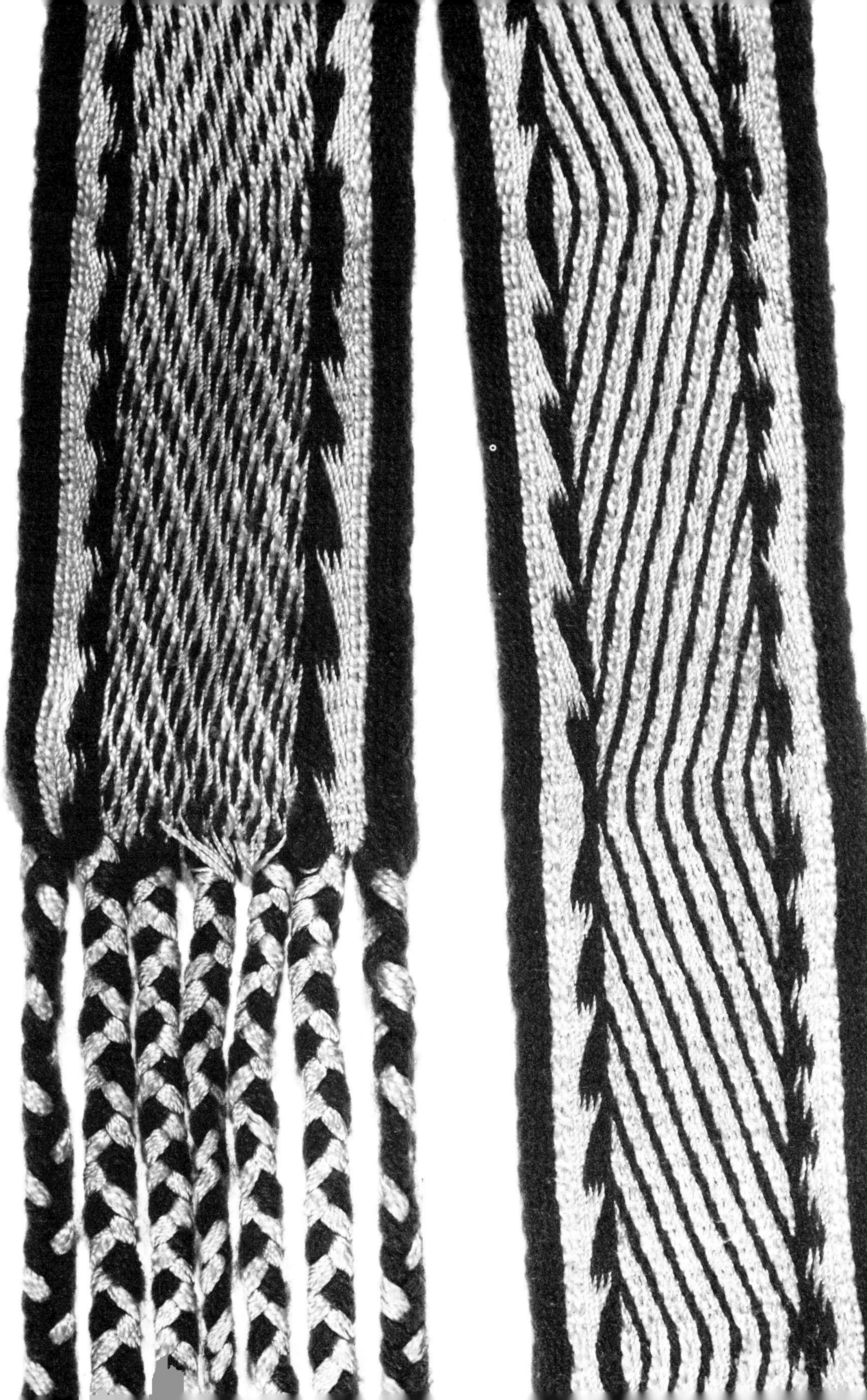

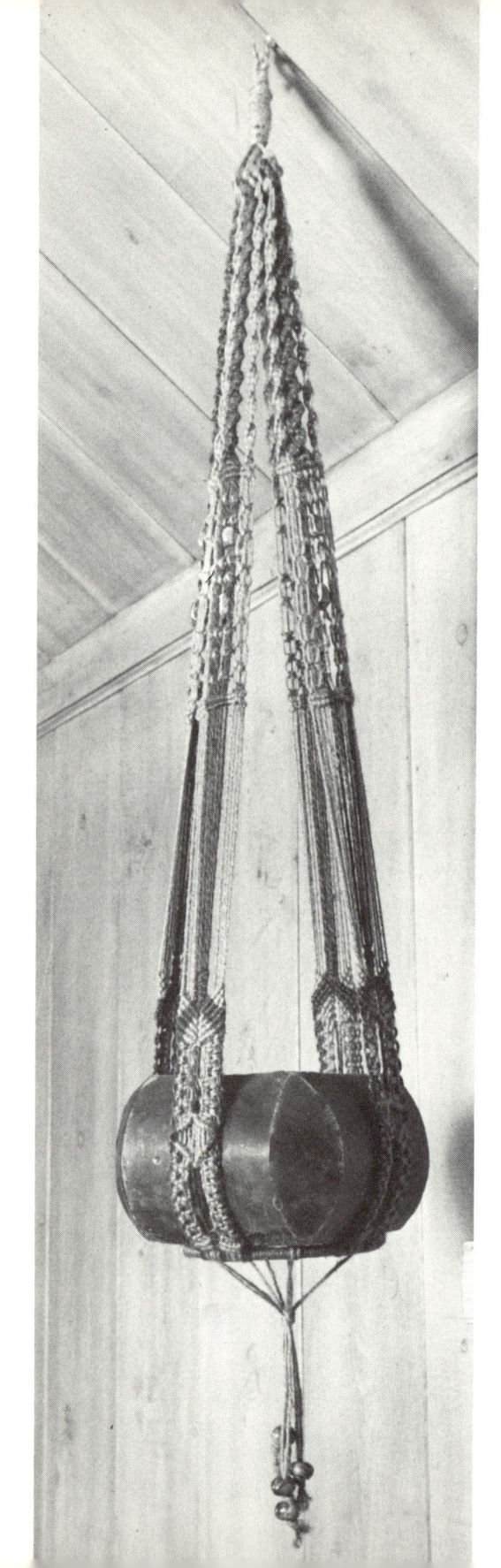

10-43. Bands make a free-swinging candleholder.

10-44. Beverly Gustavson wove an inkle band to bind the front of her hand-knit sweater.

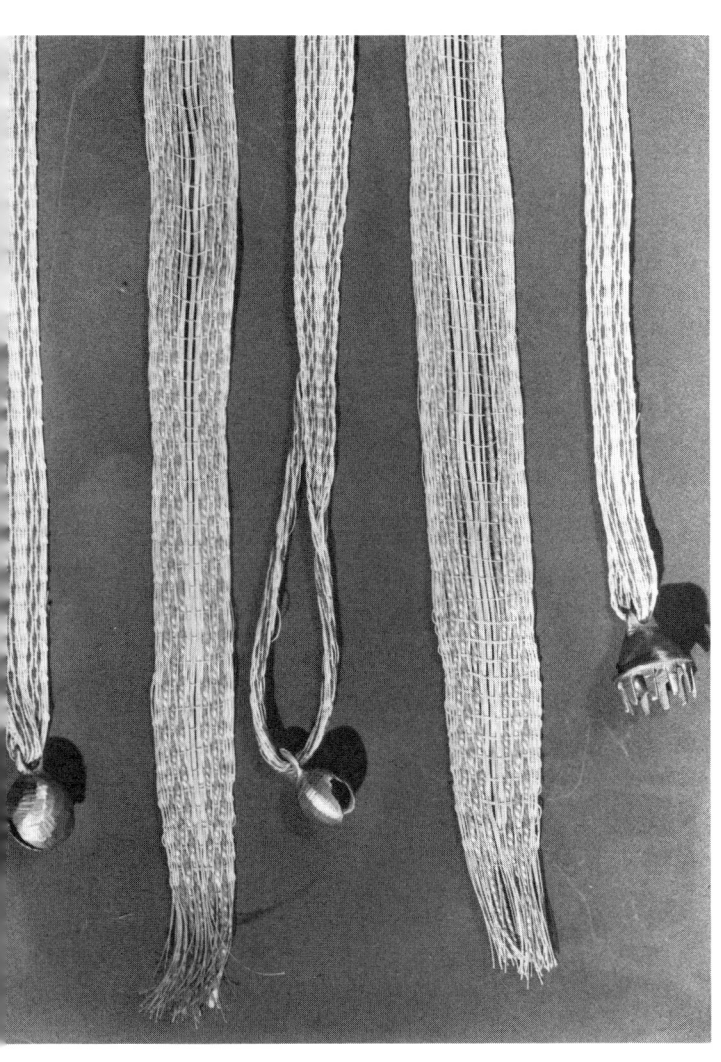

10-45. Filmy nylon bands hang in front of a window as bird warners or wind chimes.

10-46. This should give you some design ideas for band-woven trim or for a complete bag. (Courtesy of Mrs. Cyrus Dimmick.)

10-48. This tapestry, woven in a split technique, was not made of bands, but it could serve as an inspiration for a band-woven hanging. (Woven by Thurid Clark.)

10-47. The back view of a wall hanging shows how a woven band can be used to cover up a rod or dowel, as well as be part of the weaving design.

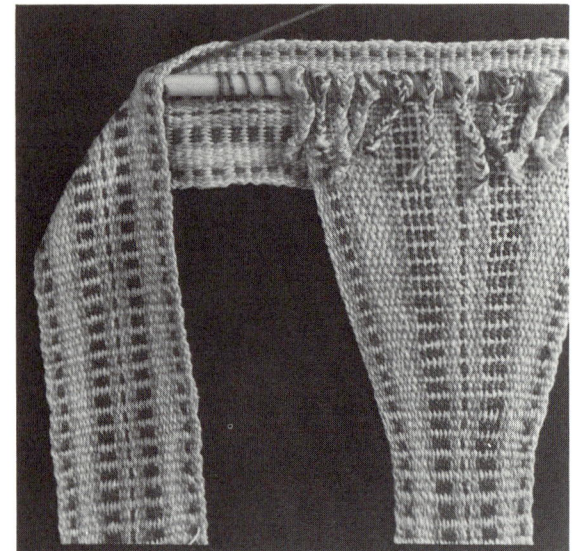

98

10-50. This rectangular garment — with a finger-woven braid for a belt — could also have been made of bands. (Woven by Harriet Gardner.)

10-49. A "memory" bag like this could be constructed with any one of the band-weaving techniques. (Woven by Thurid Clark.)

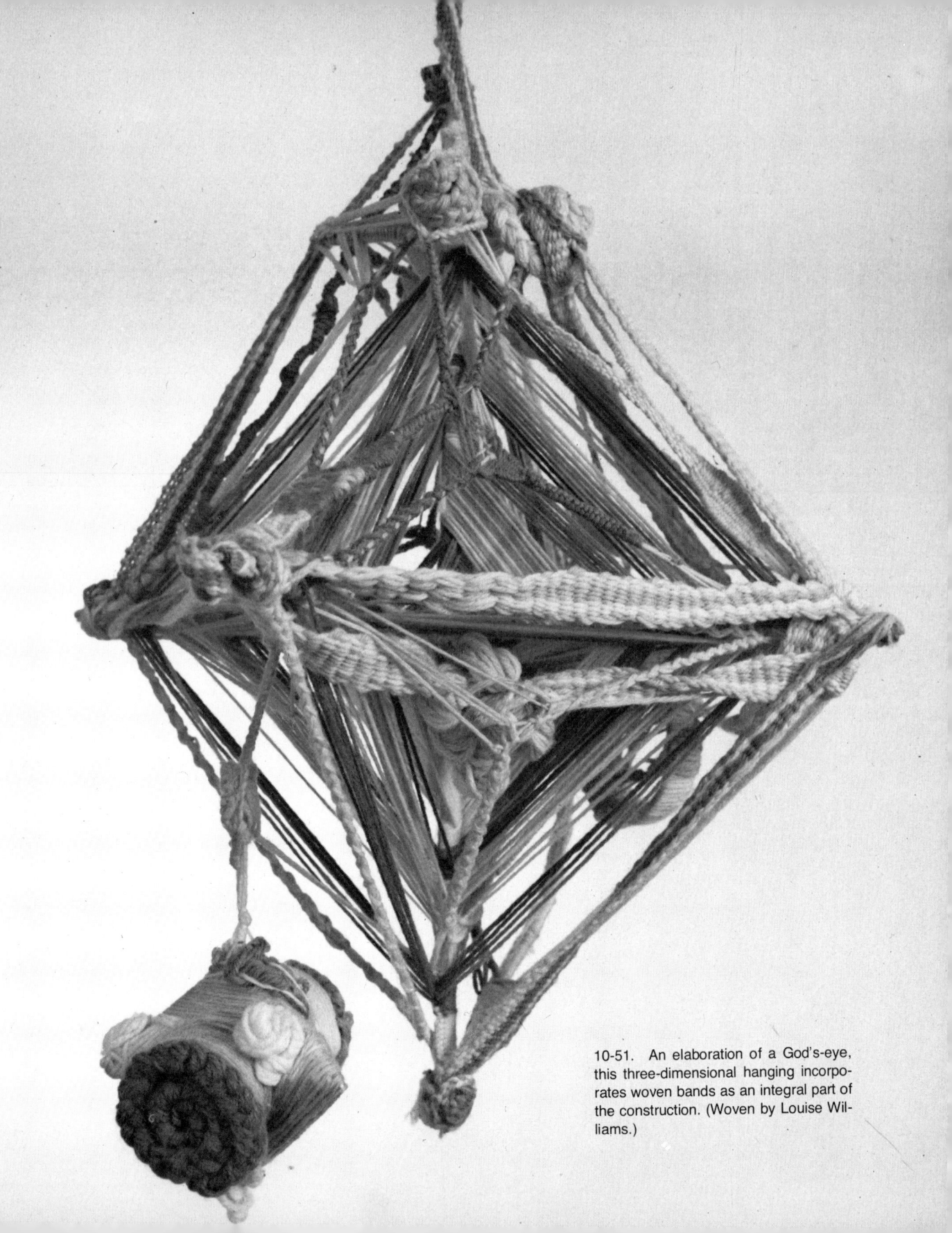

10-51. An elaboration of a God's-eye, this three-dimensional hanging incorporates woven bands as an integral part of the construction. (Woven by Louise Williams.)

list of suppliers

IN THE UNITED STATES

Yarns and Looms

Fiber to Fabric, 317 Fourth Street, Kirkland, Washington 98033.
Lily Mills, Dept. HWH, Shelby, North Carolina 28150.
Magnolia Weaving, 2635 29th West Seattle, Washington 98199.
Greentree Ranch Wools, 163 North Carter Lake Road, Loveland, Colorado 80537.
Robin and Russ, Handweavers, 533 North Adams Street, McMinneville, Oregon 97128.
The Yarn Depot, Inc., 545 Sutter Street, San Francisco, California 94102.

Yarns

Contessa Yarns, Dept. HW., PO Box 87, Lebanon, Connecticut 06349.

Looms

Schacht Spindle Company, 1708 Walnut Street, Boulder, Colorado.
Morgan Inkle Loom Factory, Railroad Engine House, Guilford, Connecticut 06437.

IN ENGLAND

Yarns

T. M. Hunter Ltd., Brora, Sutherland.
Mersey Yarns, 2 Staplands Road, Liverpool L14 3LL.
Texere Yarns, 9 Peckover Street, Bradford 1.
Yarns, 21 Postland Street, Taunton TA1 1VY
Handweavers Studio & Gallery Ltd., 29 Haroldstone Road, London E. 17 7AN.

IN CANADA AND AUSTRALIA

Yarns and Looms

South Landing Craft Centre, Queenston, Ontario.
Village Weaver, 551 Church Street, Toronto, Ontario.
Nilus LeClerc, L'Isletville, P.Q.
Art-Mat Supplies, 463 Burwood Road, Hawthorn, Victoria 3122.
Marcus Art Centre, 372 Drummond Street, Carlton, Victoria 3053.
Wondoflex Yarn Crafts, 1353 Malvern Road, Malvern, Victoria 3144.

Yarns

Yarn Mill, 438 Bloor Street West, Toronto, Ontario.
Condon's Yarns, P.O. Box 129, Charlottetown, P.E.I.
The Web, 160 Elgin Street, Place Bell Canada, Ottawa, Ontario.
Curl Bros. Textiles, 334 Lauder Avenue, Toronto, Ontario.
Loomloft Design Ltd., 300 King Street West, Toronto, Ontario.
C. M. Pullan, 48 Abell Street, Toronto, Ontario.
Walpole Wool Supply Co., P.O. Box 96, Clarkson, Ontario.
Mrs. E. Blackburn, Albion Hills Farm, R.R. 3, Caledon E., Ontario.
Golden Fleece Woollens, Box 123, Agincourt, Ontario.
Handcraft Wools, Box 378, Streetsville, Ontario.
Northwest Handcraft House Ltd., 110 West Esplanade, North Vancouver, B.C.

bibliography

Alexander, Marthann. *Weaving Handcraft*. Bloomington, Illinois: McKnight and McKnight Publishing Company, 1954. (Discussion of small looms, including a simple Hungarian loom.)

Atwater, Mary Meigs. *Byways in Handweaving*. New York: MacMillan Co., 1954. (Reliable source for unusual belt weaves.)

Bernstein, Marion H. *Off-loom Weaving*. New York: Sterling Publishing Co., 1971. (Simple sprang instructions.)

Collingwood, Peter. "Peter Collingwood, His Weaves and Weaving." Shuttlecraft monograph No. 8. Pacific Grove, California: Distributed by the Craft and Hobby Book Service, 1969.

_____*Techniques of Rug Weaving*. New York: Watson-Guptill Publishing Co., 1969. (Material on card-woven rug finish.)

Crockett, Candace. *Card Weaving*. New York: Watson-Guptill, 1973. (An excellent source for imaginative uses of card weaving.)

_____"Card Weaving." *Handweaver and Craftsman:* Summer, 1971. (A source of new ideas for card weaving.)

Groff, Russell E. *Card Weaving or Tablet Weaving*. McMinnville, Oregon: Robin and Russ Handweavers, 1969. (Source for original tablet or card weaving belt designs.)

Harvey, Virginia I. (ed.) *Threads in Action,* a quarterly publication. Box 468, Freeland, Washington 98249. (Excellent sprang instructions as well as new approaches to uses of threads.)

Harvey, Virginia I., and Tidball, Harriet. "Weft Twining." Shuttle Craft Guild Monograph No. 28. Pacific Grove, California 93950: Distributed by the Craft and Hobby Book Service.

Johnson, Pauline; Koenig, Hazel; and Moseley, Spencer. *Crafts Design*. Belmont, California: Wadsworth Publishing Corp., 1962. (Reference for inkle band weaving and for the Hungarian loom.)

Rainey, Sarita. *Weaving Without a Loom*. Worcester, Massachusetts: Davis Publishing Co., 1966. (Information about soda-straw weaving.)

Regensteiner, Elsie. *The Art of Weaving*. New York: Van Nostrand Reinhold Publishing Co., 1970. (General weaving instructions and information.)

Roth, Henry Ling. *Studies in Primitive Looms*. Halifax, England: King and Sons, Ltd., 1934 (reprint). (Delightful studies of ancient weaving tools in museum collections.)

Skowronski, Hella, and Reddy, Mary. *Sprang: Thread Twisting, a Creative Textile Technique*. New York: Van Nostrand Reinhold Co., 1973. (Detailed instructions on how to do the technique of sprang.)

Thorpe, Azalea Stuart, and Larsen, Jack Lenor. *Elements of Weaving*. Garden City, New York: Doubleday Publishing Co., 1967. (Detailed instructions for backstrap weaving.)

Tidball, Harriet. "Weaving Inkle Bands." Shuttlecraft Monograph No. 27. Pacific Grove, California: Distributed by Craft and Hobby Book Service, 1969.

Wilson, Jean. *Weaving Is Creative*. New York: Van Nostrand Reinhold Co., 1973. (Meticulous instructions for many kinds of weaving and knot-making.)

_____ *Weaving Is for anyone*. New York: Van Nostrand Reinhold Co., 1967. (Popstick and backstrap looms and weaving for children.)

_____*Weaving You can Use*. New York: Van Nostrand Reinhold Co., 1975.

index

A
area rug, 28
Atwater, Mary Meigs, 64

B
backstrap looms, 32, 41–42
bags and bag straps, 15, 16, 51, *51,*
    59, 84, 85, 97
beating in the weft shot, 13, *13*
belts, 49–50, *49,* 64, 94, 95,
bobbins, 11, *11,* 15, 16, 20, 21, 24
bookmarks, *57*
braiding, 9, *9, 14,* 14–17
broken warp threads, mending, 52–53,
    52
butterfly, yarn, 11, *11,* 15

C
card weaving, 12, *12,* 64–75, *95*
changing the shed, 9, 22, 23, *23*
    with rigid heddle, *45*
    with hands on inkle loom, 56, *57,*
        59–60
  Collingwood, Peter, 83

D
dolls, 18–19, *18,* 93
doormats, 20

E
emery board as width gauge, *10*

F
finger weaving, 14–17
four-strand braid, 14–17, *15, 16*
fringed finishes, 77–78

G
garment trim, bands for, *29, 59, 80,*
    88, 89, 96
Ghiordes knots, 78, 83, *84*
Gilmore, E. E., 54
granny knot, 47
ground shed and pattern shed, 58,
    59–60

H
heddles, 10
    rigid, 40–42 *ff.*
    weaving with two rigid, 51–52
    making, for inkle loom, 55, *55*
history of band weaving, 8–9
Hungarian loom, 11, 20–22, 30

I
Icelandic double weave, 70–71, *71*
Indians, band-weaving techniques of,
    9, 14, 26
inkle loom weaving, 10, 28, 53,
    54–55 *ff.*

J
joining bands for a mat, 23

K
knots, *17, 47, 55*

L
lark's head hitch, 17
log carrier, straps for, *92*
looms for band weaving, 9, 10, 13,
    18–19, 20–21, 26–27, 41–42,
    54–56, 64 *ff.*

M
macramé, 82

N
neckpieces, woven, *79,* 87

P
pattern shed, *see* ground shed and
    pattern shed
patterns:
    for Hungarian loom, 25, *25*
    for twining loom, *30, 31*
    for rigid heddle weaving, 53
    for inkle loom weaving, *58,* 63
    for card weaving, 74–75
pick-up patterns in inkle weaving,
    57–60, *58, 59, 60, 61*

103

pillows, *30, 91*
plaiting, 14, *and see* braiding
ponchos, *59, 86*

Q
quechquemitl, 29, *29*

R
reeds, back and front, 51–52
rigid heddle stretcher frame, 45–46, *46*
rings, weaving belt on, 49–50, *49*
ruana garment, 28, *29*

S
sandal straps, *89*
selvedges, 10, 12, 48, 55, 82
shed, 9
shed changes, *see* changing the shed
shoelaces, 69–70
shuttles, 11, *11*, 44–45, 56, 65
slits, weaving, 76
soda-straw looms, 18–19
splicing wefts, 12
sprang, *8*, 9, 82
square knot, 47
suspenders, *89*

T
tapestries, 82, *98*
tension of weft and warp, 10, 44, 50, 60, 69
   devices for creating, 15, 16, *17*, 42, *42*, 54–55, 65

thread, bubbling, *11*
tubular band weaving, *50*, 51, *83*
twining, warp, 25
   weft, 25, 26–31

W
wall hangings, 18, 19, *19*, 24–25, *24*, *60, 61, 81, 83, 98, 100*
warp-faced fabric, 9–10, *10*
warp floats, patterning with, 58–59
warp measuring devices, 43–44, 67
warp threads, 9
warp twining, card weaving as form of, 64
warp-weighted looms, 21, *21*, 82
warping a backstrap loom, 43–44
warping for card weaving, 67–68
weaving in bag handle with weft, 16
weft-faced fabric, 19
weft floats, patterning with, 62, *84*
weft fringes, 78, 82
weft threads, 9
"window weaving," *71, 72,* 72

Y
yardstick sheaths, 47–48, *47*
yarns for weaving, 15, 17, 18, 19, 20, 22, 24, 26, 29, 43, 47, 55, 62, 66
   for inkle loom heddles, 55

PHOTO CREDITS
Those photographs not included in the following list were taken by Harold and Sylvia Tacker and were printed by HELGA FORTESCUE.
KENT KAMMERER: Figures 2-2; 3-1; 5-2; 7-2; 8-11; 8-13; 8-14; 8-15; 8-16; 10-2; 10-10; 10-22; 10-25; 10-28 and 10-29; 10-32; 10-33; 10-38; 10-40; 10-43; 10-44; and 10-45.
ERNEST FORTESCUE: Figures 2-7; 8-4; 8-6; 8-7; 8-19; 9-2; 10-24; 10-37 (copy of the photograph); also C-5; C-11; C-13, and C-25 in the color section.
WILLIAM ENG: Figures 2-10; 7-7; 9-1; 10-5; 10-6; 10-7; 10-11; 10-14; and 10-42.
STEPHEN CADE: Figures 10-21 and 10-27.
JO ANN JONSON: Figure 10-36.
S. RUSSIE: Figure C-12 in the color section.
DUDLEY, HARDIN AND YANG, INC.: Figures C-15; C-20; C-22; and C-24 in the color section.

DISCARD